Praise for *Creep*

"Brilliant...a hopeful book...rooted in the steadfast belief other worlds are possible." —*The New York Observer*

"Witty, confident, and effortlessly provocative." —*The Philadelphia Inquirer*

"*Creep* is quite simply one of the best books of the decade. A truly distinctive, authentic, and dynamic literary voice...Without a doubt, *Creep* confirms that Myriam Gurba is one of our great American intellectuals, one who expertly utilizes a rapier wit to slice away the façade of hypocrisy, bigotry, bullying, and crime that marks our contemporary moment. She speaks truth to power with panache and lawyer-like logic, producing eloquent and vital essays that simultaneously provoke and entertain." —*Los Angeles Review of Books*

"Gurba writes the personal and political with invigorating conviction.... She assembles chains of seemingly unrelated memories and events whose resonances grow with each new link. She marshals myriad sources with ease and addresses difficult subjects with blunt wit.... To read Gurba at her best is to feel both the triumph of defiant self-regard as well as the soft contours of the striving it takes to acquire, preserve and restore." —*The New York Times*

"[Myriam Gurba] is the mother of intersectional Latinx identity." —*Cosmopolitan*

"Absorbing...[Gurba's] essays can be so darkly funny and artfully constructed, and she has a voice that defies how women—especially Latinx women—are expected to write/sound." —**Carolina A. Miranda**, *Los Angeles Times*

"Witty, confident, and effortlessly provocative, Gurba writes about the things that piss her off with poison and precision, sometimes daring readers to look for themselves in the tangled complicity flowchart.... *Creep* goes to some dark places, but there's something joyous about Gurba's righteous and ravenous worldview." —*The Philadelphia Inquirer*

"[*Creep*] is governed by an indomitable spirit.... Gurba catches us off guard with her unusual twinning of compassion and lacerating observation.... While these essays are full of rigorous critical thought, there's an intoxicating, lived quality to Gurba's style of analysis, her willingness to expose the funny and the cruel and the grotesque in a single breath. Gurba doesn't so much dissect her life or California history as she holds an elaborate wake, reframing our understanding of humor as a means of survival. She is an indelible contemporary voice, and we are the better for it." —**Alta Online**

"Challenging and cathartic, *Creep* is a collection of power and place, kinship and kindness, violence and atrophy. It may hurt, but this one will heal you." —**Ms.**

"Brilliant...[Gurba] skins the myth of California as a progressive playground. In its place, she offers a blistering portrait of life in the golden state.... Despite the degradations and horrors *Creep* chronicles, it's a hopeful book. A hopefulness shot through with anger, awareness, and unrest. A hope rooted in the steadfast belief other worlds are possible." —*The New York Observer*

"Haunting and otherworldly, like reading *Goosebumps* under a flashlight...With an imaginative combination of rigorous archival resources, magical realism, and wit, Gurba gives us no choice but to read on in spite of feeling spooked." —*Interview*

"Sharp, conversational cultural criticism...Gurba goes for the jugular." —**Bustle's "Best New Books for Fall"**

"Gurba is mighty. Brilliant, Mexican, wry; an ethnographer of our inheritances, she trains our eyes on the ugliness of racism, imperialism, and misogyny. A curate of liberation, Gurba pays homage to the survivors and the victims. This book is ceremony: beautiful, difficult, and important." —**Imani Perry, National Book Award–winning author of** *South to America*

"Boom! Myriam Gurba's writing is a nuclear explosion." —**Silvia Moreno-Garcia, bestselling author of** *Mexican Gothic*

Praise for *Mean*

"Gurba's 'queer art of being mean' is a triumph of deadpan humor in a timely and thrilling voice. Stop everything and read this brave and tender book." —*O, The Oprah Magazine*

"*Mean* calls for a fat, fluorescent trigger warning start to finish—and I say this admiringly. Gurba likes the feel of radioactive substances on her bare hands." —*The New York Times*

"Gurba is something of a connoisseur of cruelty. She doesn't pull her punches, but her jabs are calibrated with a perfect balance of rage and satire." —*The New York Times*

"*Mean* demands our attention not only as a painfully timely story, but also as an artful memoir.... A powerful, vital book about damage and the ghostly afterlives of abuse." —*Los Angeles Review of Books*

"With unconstrained, inventive, stop-you-in-your-tracks writing, Gurba asserts that there is glee, freedom, and, perhaps most of all, truth in meanness." —*Booklist*

"Gurba seems intent on tearing down walls and shaking readers out of complacency; her writing pulls our attention to human cruelty, suffering, and then, resilience. We are better off for it." —*BuzzFeed*

"[Gurba's skill] here is apparent in the way she demonstrates her own gradual maturing through her developing thoughts and sense of self." —*Literary Hub*

"This is a confident, intoxicating, brassy book that takes the cost of sexual assault, racism, misogyny, and homophobia deadly seriously." —*The Rumpus*

"[Gurba's] politicized consciousness comes not only through her college education, but also through the stories of the women who don't survive the violence that women of color encounter on journeys similar to hers. This is a startling and edgy book from start to finish." —*NBC News*

"[Gurba's] dark humor isn't used for shock value alone, offering instead a striking image of deflection and coping in the face of real pain and terror." —*Publishers Weekly*

Also by Myriam Gurba

Creep

Mean

Painting Their Portraits in Winter

Dahlia Season

Letter to a Bigot

POPPY STATE

POPPY

A LABYRINTH OF PLANTS AND A STORY OF BEGINNINGS

STATE

MYRIAM GURBA

TIMBER PRESS | PORTLAND, OREGON

Timber Press
Workman Publishing
Hachette Book Group, Inc.
1290 Avenue of the Americas
New York, New York 10104
timberpress.com

Timber Press is an imprint of Workman Publishing, a division of Hachette Book Group, Inc. The Timber Press name and logo are registered trademarks of Hachette Book Group, Inc.

Printed in Indiana, USA (LSC-C), on responsibly sourced paper.
Text and jacket design by Vincent James
Cover flower: Kasyanova/depositphotos.com
Cover Labyrinth: Kilroy79/VectorStock.com

The publisher is not responsible for websites (or their content) that are not owned by the publisher.

ISBN 978-1-64326-514-8

A catalog record for this book is available from the Library of Congress.

Preamble to the Author's Note

Do you like surprises?

If so, avoid the Author's Note until you are finished reading this book. However, if you are the sort of person who prefers to consult a map prior to a quest, turn to page 252.

You may read this book for the first time only once. Let that reminder inform your decision....

This is a habitat.
Life happens here.
Death does too.

"¡Que la tierra te sea leve
como tú fuiste a la tierra!"

—Ricardo Serrano Ríos

RUGGED PERENNIALS

Packets 33 cents unless otherwise specified

NATIVE SHRUBS

Packets 33 cents unless otherwise specified

DESIRABLE BULBS

Packets 33 cents unless otherwise specified

"I make a flower necklace, a flower garland, a paper of flowers, a bouquet, a flower shield, hand flowers.

    I thread them.
    I string them.
    I provide them with grass.
    I provide them with leaves.
    I make a pendant of them.
    I smell something.
    I smell them.
    I cause one to smell something.
    I cause him to smell.
    I offer flowers to one.
    I offer him flowers.
    I provide him flowers.
    I provide one with flowers.
    I provide one with a flower necklace.
    I provide him a flower necklace.
    I place a garland on one.
    I provide him a garland.
    I clothe one in flowers.
    I cover one with flowers.
    I continue to cover one with flowers.
    I cover him with flowers.
    I destroy one with flowers.
    I destroy him with flowers."

—*The Florentine Codex*

TWO TAP ROOTS: ONE PROLOGUE

"Hybrid cloud-creatures pressed in upon them, gigantic flowers with human breasts dangling from fleshy stalks, winged cats, centaurs..."

—Salman Rushdie, *The Satanic Verses*

Few flowers grew in the place where our girls-only club met, the baseball field in the southeast corner of our school playground. Bull clover sprouted along the edges of the dirt diamond, the weed's small, grimy blooms the same hue as home plate. Honeybees came for the pollen. In service of their queen, workers hovered and hummed, making music that inspired us to make-believe. World-building is most powerful when it's done with others, and my fellow visionaries were three tween tomboys who shared my appetite for ceremony, storytelling, theatricality, and adventure.

Because she was my best friend, I'll start with Charlotte. She was a contradiction, a blonde nerd. With the exception of Fortinbras, her black cat, everyone in Charlotte's family was yellow-haired and bookish. My family was nerdy too, but my father raised us to shun cats. Hamsters and snakes were our thing. Rocks and alligator lizards too.

Charlotte and I recruited Amber into our club after we saw her perform barefoot in our school talent show. Clad like a denim-loving hobo, she climbed onstage and pretended to dance in a forest. As she spun, she sang "In the Pines" a capella. When Amber twanged the lyric about feeling the cold wind blow, she pantomimed a melancholy shiver that I mimicked when stiff breezes cooled our home, the Santa Maria Valley.

Then there was Naomi, who was new to our school. It took her months to warm up to me. Once she did, she introduced me to gynecology. Her dad, a pharmacist, was also a porn enthusiast who kept a magazine stash in a cabinet beneath the bathroom sink. When her mom went to go pick up Naomi's little brother from soccer, my classmate freed her dad's collection from its hiding spot. Squatting near the toilet, we scrutinized crotches that titillated and terrified.

Our club lunched at a white picnic table wedged between the school cafeteria and a redwood tree. After finishing our sandwiches and milk, we would stampede across campus. Our sneakers and sandals carried us past drinking fountains, swing sets, handball courts, and monkey bars. The deeper into the field we ran, the greener the soles of our shoes turned. After darting into the batter box, we plopped onto its bench. It wobbled. Squeaked. Splinters pricked our butts and thighs. Instead of attributing these wounds to the unvarnished wood, we blamed them on unseen forces.

Charlotte dubbed our chosen corner Lone Pine Hill. The dugout was reborn as our "altar," "bunker," "laboratory," and "hull," the place where we connived, experimented with alchemy, and chanted in pig Latin, sacrificing whatever the entities we spoke into existence demanded of us. Some craved earthworms. Others, a paste made of ground snail, earwig, dandelion fluff, and human saliva. A bossy monster told us to fetch him a toad. A bourgeois demon could only be satisfied by a well-seasoned cracker presented to him on the biggest sycamore leaf that we could scrounge.

We spent April and May venturing to and through never-before-experienced dimensions. Unfettered by genre, the tales we wove veered from science fiction to portal fantasy to eldritch horror. Though we'd never read him, H.P. Lovecraft's spirit enlivened our games. Our improvisations summoned villains of diverse species and genders, and on a dull but sunny afternoon, Amber raised her string bean arms, threw her head back, and yodeled, "We're under attack! We're under attack!"

"Who is it?"

"A witch! Her name is...Lavinia!"

"Lavinia..." Charlotte and I echoed.

"How does Lavinia fight?" asked Naomi.

"With lightning!"

To save ourselves, we had to defeat this hag with our own electricity. Our weapon grew on the other side of the schoolyard fence. This chain link barrier separated our campus from the adult world. Just past it, a mini-Narnia tempted us to break rules.

Single-story homes and a church bordered the vacant lot. Ivy swallowed the fences protecting backyards, and what wood we could see through the waxy leaves had rotted. Storage sheds peeked across the tangled foliage. A footpath snaked through the dark soil, ending at a sidewalk. Corvids nested in the Monterey pines. Their thick boughs filtered sunlight. In the middle of this enchanted real estate, a fiery cluster of flowers blossomed.

Only a California golden poppy could neutralize Lavinia's magic.

We came up with a battle plan. Each of us had thirty seconds to dash through the gash in the chain link fence, pick a weapon, and return to the dugout with it. Failure would result in exile to another dimension. I feared what might happen to me in this one.

"My dad says it's against the law to pick those. They're our state flower," I said.

Charlotte nodded. "Yeah. I've heard that too."

Naomi fidgeted.

Amber folded her arms into wings. "You chicken?" She flapped. "Bok-bok-bok?"

I dropped to a starting position, double knotted my shoelaces, and took off. None of us were able to complete her mission in time. All four of us got booted to shittier dimensions, but the beauty of playground time is that it begins anew with each recess. The day following our banishment, we got to work creating a world without a lightning-bolt-wielding witch. We moved on to fresh challenges, and I never did tell the club why I failed at my mission.

I sabotaged myself, moving too slowly to make it to the poppies in time. Breaking plant-related laws intimidated me, and I didn't know what the police would do if I got caught with a contraband flower in my sweatpants' pocket. Weren't poppies what heroin was made of? Hadn't heroin killed John Belushi? He and Steve Martin were my dad's favorite comedians.

My father loved watching *Saturday Night Live*. He also enjoyed *America's Most Wanted*. John Walsh, a thin-lipped crimefighter, hosted the show. The FBI used it to catch fugitives, and I wondered if my mom and dad might ever be tempted to surrender me in exchange for the right reward. Further making me question my parents' loyalty was my own reaction to recent world news.

It seemed like half the planet was mad at a man named Salman Rushdie. He was a writer who'd published a novel that our elementary school library didn't carry. On TV, mobs accused the author of blasphemy. Book-burners fed his bestseller, *The Satanic Verses*, to ravenous bonfires. According to Iran's Supreme Leader, censorship was too tepid a response to Rushdie's magical realism. The Ayatollah issued a decree: *Be brave. Kill Salman.* Officials sweetened his mandate by offering a six-million-dollar bounty for the offending writer's remains.

Rushdie went into hiding, and I admit it: I fantasized about finding him and presenting his balding head to the Ayatollah. There was local precedent. In 1853, bounty hunters captured California bandit Joaquin Murrieta and decapitated him, pickling his severed head which was then exhibited up and down the state. The bounty on Murrieta was $5000, nothing compared to the one on Rushdie, and I quickly calculated how I'd spend my millions. I would tell the Iranians to wire half of my reward to my grandparents in Mexico. With that gift, I wouldn't have to worry about them being able to afford tortillas, milk, papayas, underwear, medicine, or meat. They could retire to Acapulco and hire a housekeeper. The rest of my prize would go into a college fund that I would share with my brother and sister.

When I wasn't wondering where Rushdie was, I daydreamt about being convicted of poppy-harvesting. The more elaborate the criminal punishments I thought of, the more I longed to rip these flowers out by their roots.

The taboo against picking them made these annuals ridiculously desirable. Sexy. It was the end of spring, and golden poppies were erupting from cracks in the sidewalk, taunting me. Still, the poppies that grew in our quiet valley weren't sinister. The ones that L. Frank Baum wrote about were.

I bought Baum's classic at a garage sale, and I read *The Wonderful Wizard of Oz* the way that I read most novels before I got my own room, with its spine propped against my pillow, bedsheets pulled over my head, and a plastic flashlight perched on my shoulder. In the bunk beneath mine, my asthmatic sister snored.

Honestly, I preferred the movie. Didn't you? Channel 5 aired it annually and it dragged on forever thanks to all the commercial breaks. It opens with a drab look at life on the Kansas farm where Dorothy Gale lives with her Aunt Em, Uncle Henry, and dog, Toto. Everything is sepia. Everything is sad. Dorothy's nemesis, a cyclist named Miss Gulch, pays a visit. This ugly neighbor complains to Aunt Em about being attacked by Toto and demands that the dog be put down. Despite Dorothy's threat to bite Miss Gulch, she manages to keep her canine best friend.

Bad weather steers the movie's plot toward the supernatural. When a cyclone touches down, it sucks Dorothy's house into its mouth, swishes it around, and then spits it out. The building comes crashing down in Munchkinland, and when Dorothy cautiously opens her front door, she reveals a Technicolor dream. Glinda, a good witch who travels by pink bubble, explains to Dorothy that her house has landed on the Wicked Witch of the East, crushing and killing her. This accidental assassination will likely doom Dorothy. The deceased crone is survived by her sister, the Wicked Witch of the West, and she's an even bigger asshole than her pancaked sibling.

Dorothy follows the yellow brick road in search of the wizard. He's the only one who can get her home. Along her journey, she collects three friends—the Tin Man, the Cowardly Lion, and the Scarecrow. They travel through dark and creepy woods. Mean trees pelt them with apples. Upon exiting the forest, the travelers glimpse the Emerald City glowing green in the distance. That's where the wizard lives. To reach him, Dorothy must cross a great meadow of scarlet poppies.

The friends traipse through the flowers. Dorothy is intoxicated by *Papaver somniferum*, the plant whose seeds inspired poet Elizabeth Barret Browning to write, "Opium—opium—night after night!" Lethargy sets in.

"I'm so sleepy. ..."

Toto flops on his side.

The girl from Kansas joins him.

Dorothy's friends panic.

How will they break the spell?

In her castle, the Wicked Witch of the West gazes into her crystal ball.

Her complexion is the color of fresh guacamole.

She cackles.

I, too, once fell asleep in a field of complicit flowers. My slumber happened decades after my poppy lust had cooled, and though the blooms that cushioned my outdoor bed looked like the golden poppies from my childhood, they behaved nothing like *Eschscholzia californica*. Instead, these flowers acted as accomplices to the man who transported me to them. We shall call this suitor my marijuana prince.

Steve, one of my community garden neighbors, set me up with the guy. My friend Marta and I tended a plot where we grew chiles, artichokes, tomatoes, beans, beats, squash, carrots, cilantro, and onions. In his plot, Steve mostly grew ornamental flowers, a brazen violation of community garden policy which he never seemed to get in trouble for. The rules said that we were supposed to devote three-fourths of our land to growing edible stuff. Technically, peonies are edible but consuming them will disrupt your social life. They can trigger a rash, rile up your stomach, and turn your colon spastic.

As an adult, I'd continued to practice 'girls only' policies. I primarily applied them to dating. I eased these restrictions when I entered a dry spell, a romantic drought, and so when Steve told me that a friend of his had seen me around the community garden and had a little crush on me, I perked up.

I was curious. What might it be like to spend private time with someone who could inflate a mushroom between his legs? I would find out.

The marijuana prince and I texted, and he suggested that we meet on a Thursday afternoon, at a beach parking lot. When I arrived, I found him leaning against a scruffy palm tree, clutching a bouquet of bird of paradise. "For you," he said, handing the gift to me. Then, he unloaded a picnic basket and tablecloth from his Jeep.

"I hope you like carbs," he said.

I laughed. The unoriginal joke disarmed me.

We walked toward the ocean until the marijuana prince ordered, "Stop." Then, he unfurled the tablecloth across the sand, securing its corners with rocks. Across our makeshift table he arranged a baguette, a stick of butter, brie, red grapes, a bar of dark chocolate, plates, wine glasses, napkins, and a knife. We sipped Chianti, buttered our bread, and watched pelicans dive for fish. Glowing like a fat, ripe strawberry, the sun half sank into the Pacific.

The marijuana prince reached into his shirt pocket and pulled out a glass pipe. At first, I thought it was mushroom-shaped. When I realized that it was phallic instead of fungal, I blushed. Next, he reached into his jeans pocket and fished out a black film canister. He popped it open, took a pinch, and nestled the herb in the bowl, tapping it three times with his index finger. After producing a lighter, he fired up, put lips to the pipe, and inhaled for what seemed like a superhuman amount of time. Before I could say excuse me, he'd grabbed me and kissed me, exhaling, infusing my body with THC. Smoke curled down my throat and into my lungs, caressing my alveolar sacs.

I quickly became addicted to the scent of the marijuana prince. He smelled of coconut. Clove. Vanilla. Cinnamon. Cardamom.

He was a stoner pastry.

I gave up sleeping in my own bed so that I could wake to his intoxicating aroma.

This pleased him.

"I want you here all of the time," he said. "I want you to stay with me."

When we'd been seeing each other for about three months, the marijuana prince told me something concerning. "I've been waiting for someone like you all my life. I'd almost given up." A tear rolled down his fragrant cheek. "Every woman I've ever loved has betrayed me. I know that you won't."

His words chilled me, but I stayed. I didn't want to bring him more pain.

The following Saturday, after we'd eaten toasted ham and cheese croissants on his patio, the marijuana prince announced that we would drive to the high desert, to a valley where pronghorn antelope once ran wild among the Joshua trees. Destiny had chosen this landscape for a superbloom, a spectacle of wildflowers that Californians were clamoring to see. Heavy winter rains and long-dormant seeds had made this rare event possible, and our journey would take us near Lancaster, the town where the Gumm Sisters had entertained locals by performing song and dance routines at the Valley Theatre. Baby Gumm was the youngest sister, and her father, Jack, operated the theatre. He leased it but was run out of town once the community discovered his secret.

Jack liked boys.

He hired them as ushers and (rumor was) he tried ushering himself into their laps.

The Gumm Sisters performed up and down the West Coast, but critics liked Baby best. Her big break arrived in 1935. On September 13, the thirteen-year-old auditioned for MGM studios. They offered her a seven-year contract, billing the Lancaster girl as Judy Garland. Before she'd go on to star in *The Wizard of Oz*, the future Dorothy would experience a loss that she considered her life's great tragedy. Her dad died. At his funeral, Baby locked herself in the bathroom. It was her first time seeing someone in a casket, and the actor was ashamed that she couldn't make herself cry.

One of my dad's sisters lived in Lancaster. During a visit, she'd taken me on a driving tour. When we cruised past 44665 Cedar Avenue, my aunt said, "That's where Judy Garland lived." I gasped at how ordinary Dorothy's childhood home looked. I guess I was expecting Munchkinland.

I figured that the marijuana prince and I would see lots and lots of bright colors during our visit to the superbloom. The drive to the Mojave lasted hours. We parked on a soft dirt shoulder. Clear sky greeted us. The wind blew hard, threatening to pluck petals and send them sailing. We climbed a gentle slope blanketed by golden poppies.

"Lie down," ordered the marijuana prince. "I'll take your picture."

Not wanting to be like the other women who'd hurt him, I obeyed. My weight crushed petals and stems. The marijuana prince snapped photos that I never saw and now, when I shut my eyes to envision them, I conjure a short-haired Ophelia, eyes shut, lips slightly parted, a pair of turkey vultures circling overhead.

I look dead.

Maybe I was.

The flowers had anaesthetized me, forcing my eyelids shut and then paralyzing me. Like Dorothy, I slept. Unlike Dorothy, I remained that way for a very long time, my soul travelling to other dimensions, realms haunted by absinthe drinkers, zombies, and Death. This skeletal doula caressed my cheeks with her bony fingers, and when I'd begin to stir, threatening to wake up, her skull would descend, nearing my lips. She planted calcified kisses on me and blew fine graveyard dust into my mouth.

My soul wandered for three years. That was how long it took for me to be rescued from the marijuana prince and his botanical accomplices.

In *The Wizard of Oz*, Dorothy's friends cry for help and are heard by Glinda. She whips up some good magic, making it snow. The sudden drop in temperature wakes Dorothy. The moisture causes the Tin Man to rust and freeze.

I was roused by the hum of an air conditioner. When I opened my eyes, I saw Juan Gabriel, Marta's Persian cat, perched on a tattered couch arm. Marta, Juan Gabriel, and I never discussed those three lost years. It was too terrifying to admit that I'd been played by a man-witch.

We pretended that my poppy coma hadn't happened.

We treated my lost years like seeds, burying them.

I took up temporary residence in Marta's spare room, one she planned on someday using as a nursery. The space felt right. I was a baby learning to walk and talk and eat again. I was also as scared of being alone as I was of becoming a burden. Having spent years cradled by Death, I rejected solitude, overstaying my welcome everywhere I visited. Supermarkets. Pharmacies. Thrift stores. Churches.

Once Marta got pregnant, I decided to leave the nursery, hopping from mattress to couch to mattress to floor. I became expert at packing and hasty evacuations. It seemed impossible for me to put down roots. I travelled so lightly that it still sometimes seemed that I was as dead as my Mexican and Polish grandfathers.

...azquil azquil azquil azquil
azquil azquil azquil azquil
azquil azquil azquil azquil
azquil azquil azquil azquil
azquil azquil azquil azquil azquil azquil azquil azquil azquil azquil azquil
azquil azquil azquil azquil azquil azquil azquil azquil azquil azquil...

...azquil azquil azquil azquil azquil azquil azquil azquil azquil azquil azquil
azquil azquil azquil azquil azquil azquil azquil azquil azquil azquil azquil
azquil azquil azquil azquil azquil azquil azquil azquil azquil azquil azquil
azquil azquil azquil azquil...

...azquil azquil azquil azquil azquil azquil azquil azquil azquil
azquil azquil azquil azquil azquil azquil azquil azquil azquil azquil azquil
azquil azquil azquil azquil azquil azquil azquil azquil azquil azquil azquil
azquil azquil azquil azquil azquil azquil...
...azquil azquil azquil azquil azquil azquil azquil
azquil azquil azquil azquil azquil azquil azquil azquil azquil azquil azquil
azquil azquil azquil azquil azquil azquil azquil azquil azquil azquil azquil
azquil azquil azquil azquil azquil azquil azquil azquil...

...azquil azquil azquil azquil azquil azquil azquil azquil azquil azquil azquil
azquil azquil azquil azquil azquil azquil azquil azquil azquil azquil azquil
azquil azquil azquil azquil azquil azquil azquil azquil azquil azquil azquil
azquil azquil azquil azquil...

...azquil azquil azquil azquil azquil azquil
azquil azquil azquil azquil azquil azquil azquil azquil
azquil azquil azquil azquil azquil azquil azquil azquil
azquil azquil azquil azquil azquil azquil azquil azquil
azquil azquil azquil azquil azquil azquil azquil...

...ants...

"'How queer!' said the yellow hen. 'Do you think that is all true, my dear?'"

—L. Frank Baum, *Ozma of Oz*

The difference between grasshoppers and locusts is attitude. Grasshoppers are loners. They revel in solitude and silence, demanding no audience. Locusts, on the other hand, are grotesquely gregarious. As these bugs coalesce, they rub exoskeletons, triggering a collective ecstasy that shifts the meaning of the term "contact high." They travel by swarm, moving as a singular, ravenous entity capable of eclipsing celestial bodies such as the sun, the moon, and the Goodyear Blimp.

A locust's presence is always plural.

In 1931, locusts ravaged the American Midwest, gobbling crops, lumber, and leather. They dined on homesteads till only glass and zippers were left. Photographs of the devastation published by small town newspapers are reminiscent of the Kansas farm where *The Wizard of Oz* begins. To escape this winged horror, farmers abandoned their lands and moved west. Many came to California. Here, new nightmares awaited them.

Psychoanalyst Alfred Ernest Jones, a friend and biographer of Sigmund Freud, wrote beautifully about nightmares. In a monograph devoted to the subject, he noted that "it has long been recognized that even in the most terrifying nightmares, the angst often has a distinctly traceable voluptuous character." Jones' description evokes glamour. It almost makes me want to have a nightmare.

Almost.

I suffered from chronic nightmares following my poppy-induced slumber. Residual intoxicants influenced them. These bad dreams attacked like locusts, devouring hope, obscuring daylight, and reminding me of Death. In the worst ones, I smell coconut. Vanilla. Cinnamon. Cardamon.

The sensation of skin pressed against skin.

His hands.

My neck.

A grip and a squeeze and out slips my soul, looking like a scrap of pale tulle exiting my mouth.

I watch her float away....

She cuts a wan silhouette against black velvet sky before dipping into the fog.

In this haze, mosquitos buzz.

Bullfrogs croak.

Whippoorwills chant their name.

Marsh grasshoppers rub leg against wing.

Rasp.

Rasp.

Rasp.

The haze dissipates. A swamp illuminated by fireflies materializes.

From a thicket of bulrush, a skeletal hand waves.

It's Death. She's crouched in the cattails, waiting.

Without a body to channel my panic, I hover like a fool.

In these nightmares, I'm often not in California, and my soul has roamed as far away as Massachusetts, land of Emily Dickinson, Cotton Mather, and clam chowder. On rare nights, my soul returns to the house where my father and I planted oak trees and coyote brush. Without hands, it's impossible for my spirit to bring me back a souvenir, a reminder of home.

An acorn. A scrap of snakeskin. A skunk whisker.

A dab of Vicks VapoRub.

Desperate for a good night's sleep, I sought out a home. A real one, not someone else's couch, futon, lumpy spare mattress, or nursery. I figured that maybe, if I rooted myself somewhere, my subconscious would quit terrorizing me. I had to give my soul a reason to stop wandering. My body could better house my spirit if she also had a real home.

I scoured property management websites, made a phone call, and drove to a quiet, jacaranda-lined street. These same trees also flanked the front walk of the fortress-like stucco building that I'd come to tour, and I pretended that the lilac flowers which stuck to the concrete leading to the gate had been strewn for me. A building manager named Dolores showed me a second-floor corner unit. When she asked if I was interested, I answered, "I'll take it."

Moving in was easy. I furnished my one-bedroom apartment with hand-me-downs and junk scavenged from the alley below my bedroom window. I'm seated at the table pushed against the dining room picture window. I gaze at garage doors. Parking lots. An orange and white cat napping in the shadow of a blue dumpster.

I admire the way morning glory drapes itself across a fence.

I lean on my elbow and tilt my tired face toward the sun.

I pretend I'm a leaf.

Una hoja.

Hojalá.

I share this apartment with plants.

That means that I also share it with bugs.

At sunset, crickets squeeze through a crack in my kitchen wall, invading.

I've asked them to be quiet, but they ignore me.

My indoor garden and I have resigned ourselves to their nocturnal chamber music.

Have you ever fantasized about planting a corn maze in your living room? This unorthodox idea was inspired by the spirit of my great-grandmother, a prolific indoor gardener.

It was also inspired by cannabis.

I got the idea for the indoor maize labyrinth as I was puffing away at a marijuana cigarette, tapping the cherry against the lip of an empty can of refried beans. This is how I spend my evenings. Sharing hare-brained schemes with the moon and exposing my photosynthetic roommates to secondhand smoke.

Roommates isn't quite the right word to describe who plants are to me.

It'll have to do for now.

During the glory days of the Lone Pine Hill dugout, my mother encouraged me to read books written by Frances Hodgson Burnett. Mom loved *A Little Princess*. It was alright. I liked *The Secret Garden* better. Mary, its hero, gets orphaned and is sent to live with an uncle whose manor house is in the Yorkshire moors. Mary makes an unlikely friend and the two of them create their own version of Lone Pine Hill, a two-kid club that makes mystics out of both children. Through gardening and play, the fractured pair become whole again.

In my apartment, I work on doing the same, and while my mom was the one who indirectly introduced me to the idea of a secret garden capable of restoration, it was my dad who mentored me in botany, horticulture, and natural history, encouraging my affection for flora and plant-adjacent life-forms. I fell in love with some of the leafy beings that he and I planted, and from him, I learned how to tell the difference between plants who are friends and those who are potential enemies.

I should never have trusted that peony grower.

Steve.

The roommates took over my apartment quickly.

African violets were the first to make themselves at home.

They preened for my attention from their rack at the 99 Cents Only Store. A handwritten sign said that they were priced at three dollars each, and I deliberated while standing at the checkout line, waiting to pay for a basketful of cheap household-starter goods.

"Could you hold my place?" I asked the bearded customer behind me.

He nodded. I scurried to the violets and carried as many as I could back to the line.

At home, I placed a violet on my bedroom dresser and another on my dining room table. The smallest one went on a ledge in my bathroom. The violets didn't cure my nightmares, but they provoked something I hadn't experienced in years—enthusiasm for being alive. I *wanted* to wake up in the morning. Dawn signaled that it was time to throw off my covers and dash to my violets. It was my responsibility to make sure that their soil remained damp, and I was dying to watch them unfurl their petals and show off their different shades of pink and purple.

I returned to the 99 and splurged, purchasing a dozen problem plants, vegetative gargoyles who needed to be reminded of their worth. In their unhappiness, they looked evil. With care, their ugliness softened. I put to work the lessons my dad had taught me. Their beauty returned.

Plants cover most of my dining room table. Kale grows in a plastic tub. Squash is her neighbor. Wormwood splays lacy fingers. Honeysuckle reaches for the light. Chamomile perfumes. Rue protects. I could go into detail about the sunflowers, the marigolds, the roses, the aloe, the mint, the ferns, and the tobacco, but for now, I'll wait.

Instead, I want to show you something on my kitchen windowsill—a dented can of El Pato brand enchilada sauce filled with courtyard dirt. My brother mailed me a packet of California golden poppy seeds about a month ago, and I buried a few in the can.

They've sprouted!

I'm trying to grow my own weapon. My own poppy.

When this flower arrives, I will not sabotage myself. I'll nurture that bloom, I'll pick her and I'll use her magic to vanquish the stoner sorcery that continues to hurt me. My dad taught me not to pick these flowers, but he also taught me how to care for them. I spent my childhood watching him be the best version of himself when his hands were plunged in soil.

I am his dirt daughter.

"Landscapes have interlocking sets of locations which are holy in and of themselves because they are the most specific means whereby the earth can relate to lesser entities."

—Vine Deloria Jr.

MAÍZ

It would've been painfully corny to begin by welcoming you into my secret garden, but now that you're here, wandering my furrows, I can finally whisper, "Bienvenide. Try the huitlacoche."

This is my conceptual corn labyrinth, a maize maze that I'm watering with blood, tears, sweat, saliva, Coca Cola, Nespresso, and Gatorade.

I tell this garden, this maze, into existence. My mouth plants it.

My tongue plows it.

My fingers hoe it.

I'm not the first woman in my family to do something like this.

We have an agricultural history. We know grain. We know corn.

Corn knows us.

My great-grandfather Gumecindo grew her the traditional way.

He also built his house, his jacal, the traditional way.

At the edge of a cliff, he fashioned four walls out of wood, stone, and mud. Next, he fashioned a roof with palm thatch. The home's floor existed before its walls or roof did.

She was earth. Dirt. Humus. Loam. Soil. Nutritious. Delicious. Mother. Earth.

My grandfather Ricardo was born on the cliff where Gumecindo built their nest. I think of their jacal as a nest because of its palm thatch.

East of the cliff where my grandfather learned to crawl stands Azqueltán, a village whose Tepecano name means "place of the ants."

In Azqueltán, people honor corn as kin. She's edible mother.

Starch mamá.

Azqueltán's insectile name recalls how the community once was. Bustling. From afar, the constant streams of people coming and going, coming and going, coming and going, created the illusion of a teeming ant metropolis.

...azquil....   ...azquil....   ...azquil....

In 1910, zoologist William Morton Wheeler delivered a lecture titled "The Ant Colony as Organism." He told his fellow biologists that he recognized ant colonies—which I prefer to call ant communities—as superorganisms. Wheeler likened the ant colony to a cell or a person, an entity that "behaves as a unitary whole, maintaining its identity in space, resisting dissolution and, as a general rule, any fusion with other colonies of the same or alien species."

My mom calls ants azquiles.

Azquiles trigger her bloodthirst.
    I've watched her smash them dead with her thumbs.
    She's shorter than five feet, but to the azquiles, my mother is Godzilla.

My mom hates the work of toy entrepreneur Milton Levine, creator of Uncle Milton's Ant Farm. I wanted one of Levine's kits for Christmas but never found one under our tree. Levine began selling his fad product in 1956, advertising it on TV. His farm's residents, California harvester ants, were sent to kids by mail. The container where the bugs dug their civilization was transparent, allowing voyeurs to peer at the ants doing things that the kit's packaging promised: "building bridges," "digging subways," "moving mountains." When I saw ant farms at our local toy store, I fixated on them, staring, watching the bugs move through their subterranean labyrinths. Seeing them exposed this way made me feel as if I knew their secrets.

The Minotaur roamed one of the most famous labyrinths, the maze built by Daedulus for King Minos. Part man and part bull, the Minotaur ate people for breakfast, lunch, and dinner. He left messy piles of bone, hair, and toga.

Proceed with caution. Hungry creatures also live in this habitat.

If you treat the hungry creatures that live here with respect (and by respect, I mean that you offer them a little something to eat, drink, or smoke) you should be fine.

In Azqueltán, thirsty people once showed respect to water spirits by offering four splashes of pinole.

One to the north.

One to the west.   One to the east.

One to the south.

These water spirits, which protect many Mexican estuaries, are called chanes. They're enormous serpentine creatures that fly. Horns sprout from their heads and they may simulate the appearance of rainbows; red, orange, yellow, green, blue, and indigo stripes band their flexible bodies.

Like my childhood hamster, a chan will attack when bothered.

When drinking water from a stream, a thirsty traveler may prevent a chan bite by using her hands as a cup, rather than putting her lips to the water's surface.

Those who are wounded by these flying snakes are encouraged to seek the services of a spiritual healer.

At the dawn of the twentieth century, about half of the people living in Azqueltán streamed out, re-settling elsewhere.

Corn had grown too expensive.

About twenty-five years later, my great-grandparents strapped their possessions to their donkeys, walked to Guadalajara, and abandoned their cliff.

Corn had grown too expensive.

In Guadalajara, my great-grandparents sold Coca Cola. They never did return to growing corn. Maize, however, found her way into soft drinks.

In 1980, Coca Cola began replacing cane sugar with high-fructose corn syrup.

It is correct to say that chemists Richard Marshall and Earl Kooi invented corn syrup in Argo, Illinois.

It is incorrect to say that corn originated in Mexico, though people say so all the time.

Mexico is two hundred and three years old. Corn is ten thousand years old. That makes corn nine thousand seven hundred and ninety-seven years older than Mexico.

Before corn was corn, she was teosinte, a wild grass that sprouted cute little cobs bearing about a dozen hard kernels.

Ancient humans domesticated these meager ears, breeding teosinte so that it swelled, encouraging cobs to grow long, thick, and corny.

After studying corn's ancestry, geneticists determined that four or five long-ago mutations transformed teosinte into maize.

Most of this genetic research was conducted in American laboratories.

The United States of America consumes, produces, and exports more corn than any country in the world, including Mexico.

Most of this corn is genetically engineered.

In 2020, Mexico issued a decree outlawing the use of genetically engineered corn for human consumption. This prohibition pissed off American corn farmers who argued that "the science overwhelmingly shows that genetically modified corn is safe for consumers and does not harm native plants."

GMO apologists are full of it.

By "it" I mean caca.

Mundo Maíz, Latin America's largest corn maze, grows in Tlaquepaque, Jalisco. It's more than twenty acres of sweaty corn.

Aerial shots of it look like a Led Zeppelin album cover.

Mundo Maíz is not to be confused with Mundo Elote, a Tlaquepaque food store that primarily sells corn.

According to *The Guadalajara Reporter*, Mundo Maíz offers something called "an extreme zone." This attraction caters to tourists "seeking a more intensive thrill…"

There's also something called a "zombie challenge" that happens on weekends, beginning at 6:30 pm.

Cornfields can be terrifying.

In 1977, during the month of March, *Penthouse Magazine* published "Children of the Corn," a short story by Stephen King.

Two months later, I was born.

In "Children of the Corn," Burt and Vicky, a married couple, bicker in their car. They're driving across land that's flat and uninhabited.

They're headed for my home. California.

In Nebraska, Burt hits a boy darting out of a cornfield.

The couple pulls over.

They park.

Burt and Vicky enter the cornfield.

Spoiler alert.

They never make it to California.
They become friends of Dorothy.
Scarecrows.

My cornfield is unlike Stephen King's. Exiting my maize maze is easy. Step away from the story and, like a chan—poof—it's gone.

It's not the same for me.

I can't leave until I'm ready.

And that depends on the poppy in the enchilada sauce can resting on my kitchen windowsill.

When will she be ready?

Turning pages twists the reader's path.
She must get lost to get unlost.

OUR WILDFLOWERS. Seven Different
Varieties Named and Described as They Come.

Santa Maria Times, Saturday, March 12, 1892

Having been requested by the editors of the Times *to contribute a few articles on the wildflowers of the Santa Maria Valley, it seems timely to begin now, while the early flowers are with us, to describe those in bloom, giving technical names and medicinal or other economic uses when known....*

ERYTHEA

When I was fifteen, I practiced a taboo religion: lesbianism. Fern, a fellow Catholic schoolgirl who lived in a whitewashed farmhouse, worshipped with me.

We trysted in our local cemetery. We wandered its hushed grounds, held hands, kissed, and admired headstones. We especially liked the weathered ones, markers that were cracked, mossy and askew. We brought our clandestine romance to the graveyard because we assumed its skeletal residents wouldn't tattle on us. We were wrong. The Santa Maria Cemetery has two known chatterboxes. One doesn't hide it. She expresses herself through her tombstone.

A settler of German descent, Margaret Rector Turman Winn was born in Pennsylvania in 1784. She collected many husbands, birthed fourteen children, and traveled to California by wagon train. In 1875, at age ninety, she died a widow many times over. A nosegay is etched at the top of her fallen and fractured headstone. A creed is etched across the bottom: "Spiritualism is no delusion but a demonstrated fact."

I learned about this demonstrated fact, and the messy seances it inspired, from books I found shelved in our town library's occult corner. A metaphysical movement whose participants channel and speak with the deceased, spiritualism was once so popular that heads of state dabbled in it. Mexican President Francisco I. Madero was a staunch vegetarian who developed a skill popular among spiritualists—automatic writing. This act allows the deceased to commandeer a living hand, enabling spirit to animate warm flesh. Raúl, the President's little brother who died by fire at age four, authored Madero's earliest spiritist jottings.

After the death of her eleven-year-old son, Willie, First Lady Mary Todd Lincoln held seances in the Red Room of the White House. Mediums succeeded at contacting her son, and Mrs. Lincoln confided to her sister that at night, Willie would materialize at the foot of her bed, smiling. Sometimes, he brought a companion, Eddie, his four-year-old brother who'd coughed himself to death.

On the evening of April 14, 1865, while the First Lady and President sat side by side in the balcony of Ford's Theatre, an assassin crept behind them. The killer drew his derringer, aiming it at Abraham Lincoln's head. The shot that was fired emancipated the President's brain. A few years later, William Mumler took Mrs. Lincoln's final portrait at one of his spirit-photography studios. In the albumen silver print, the widow sits. Behind her hovers her spectral husband. His large diaphanous hands rest on her shoulders.

Eleazar "Lazar" Emanuel Blochman is the other Santa Maria Cemetery denizen open to posthumous chitchat. Born in 1856, Lazar was the son of a San Francisco milkman and his milliner wife. He arrived in this valley in 1882, and while he prospered here, Lazar did not cherish this place. "When I came to Santa Maria," the aspiring meteorologist wrote in his diary, "it was a hamlet of less than five hundred inhabitants, with no paved streets, no gardens and no social life such as I had enjoyed before."

Two years after his arrival, while serving as a board of education trustee, Lazar met someone enjoyable. Ida Mae Twitchell was a thirty year-old college graduate who taught at La Graciosa, a rustic campus with a redwood schoolhouse that could accommodate no more than sixty students. Originally from Maine, Ida looked the part of the stern schoolmarm. She wore high-necked black dresses and squinted through pince-nez. Those who knew her claim she was fun. Members of the local historical society tell the following anecdote to demonstrate just how fun she was.

The possibility that trouble might find Ida worried her brother. Each morning and afternoon, she plodded alone alongside the railroad tracks to get to and from school. He insisted that Ida carry something to protect herself with, and she accepted the firearm that he gave her, always carrying it with her. She doubted that she could use it to kill a man, but she kept it on her to please her family. She was comfortable cutting short the life of a daisy, but a human being?

Never.

One school day, after the lunch bell had clanged, a group of older boys began yelling at each other, tussling over teen things. Instead of breaking up the fight, Ida placed her basket on her desk. This gesture caught the boys' attention, and they watched her open its lid and reach inside. After removing some papers, which she set on her desk, Ida reached for her gun and set it on top of the sheaf. The boys froze. Their eyes followed Ida's hands as she took out her lunch pail and then replaced her papers and pistol. Next, she pried open her pail and got out her food.

The schoolmarm chewed in silence. Students never got rowdy around her again.

In college, Ida had majored in botany, and her enthusiasm for accumulating plant knowledge persisted after she was handed her diploma. Ida hunted for plant specimens with Alice Eastwood, a fellow schoolteacher who would become head of the California Academy of Sciences's botany department. The friends went camping in Cuyama. They also explored Zaca Lake, a place that has long scared local kids. *Friday the 13th* and *Creature from the Black Lagoon* were filmed there. During one of their botanizing trips, Eastwood "discovered" California pitcher sage, a ridiculously fragrant plant with soft pink flowers that squish like snapdragons. Eastwood dubbed her find *Sphacele blochmanae*, but Ida's name didn't stick. The plant's Linnaean classification is *Lepechinia calycina*, a Russian derived name.

Lazar and Ida married in 1888. Fascinated by weather phenomena and prognostication, Lazar spent his spare time carefully studying the Santa Maria Valley's fog and precipitation. Bothered by the absence of trees, he worked to fix the problem, raising and planting eucalyptus, cypress, and pine. Impressed by Ida's botanical expertise, editors at the *Santa Maria Times* invited her to contribute a regular column.

"Our Wildflowers" debuted in March of 1892, with Ida devoting most of her first installment to the poppy family. She boasts that *Papaver*'s "most brilliant representative is the well-known 'California Poppy,' and she concludes by suggesting a questionable home remedy for indigestion, wild peony tea. In ensuing years, Ida would publish a series of articles about native plants in *Erythea*, a botanical journal whose 1893 edition included an entry for *Senecio blochmaniae*, a tufted perennial plentiful along the Santa Maria River that was named for her. That same year, at the World's Fair in Chicago, Ida exhibited her herbarium, which consisted of six hundred plants culled from northern Santa Barbara County. This herbarium became the property of Northwestern University, and I figure its specimens are pretty crunchy by now.

Ida's wildflower column encouraged readers to embrace "our indigenous plants." She argued that these beings are "well worthy of introduction to our gardens," where they might prove "interesting and beautiful..." Ida's authorial voice blends the scientific with the folksy, and she demonstrated a talent for expressing plant character and temperament. These qualities are evident in her description of *Claytonia perfoliata*, a weed that my mom and dad have always called verdolaga: "A plant popularly known as 'Wild Lettuce' has been in bloom a month or more...it is a succulent herb and thrives best in moist shady places; it is often found under the Live Oaks...It is sometimes used as a pot-herb and children eat the juicy stems. I asked one boy how they tasted, and he said, 'no they aren't peppery but watery and have a sort of twang to them."

Twangy herbs. What a great name for a country band.

Ida worked to cultivate a passion for botany in young people. Plants were woven into her pedagogy. On the grounds of the high school, she supervised a group of students who designed, selected, and planted a garden of "choice flowers" and "rare plants." She cautioned kids against befriending dangerous plants, like tobacco. In 1889, at a meeting of the Teacher's Institute of Los Angeles County, she described *Nicotiana* as a creature "lying in wait to steal the health and physique of schoolboys." She took her vilification a little too far when she slurred tobacco, calling the gift an "evil" weed.

Shortly after Ida and Lazar married, they adopted Harry Ecklind, the orphaned son of Swedish immigrants. The new parents' joy didn't last long. Ida's wildflower column ceased publication after Harry was found dead in a beanfield. On July 6, 1901, two brothers spied the thirteen-year-old's remains from the road. When police examined his body, they tallied nine stab wounds. The *Santa Maria Times* described the murder as "one of the most infamous crimes ever recorded in this section of our state." The *San Francisco Chronicle* called it "the most fiendish murder ever known in these parts." In 1906, William Kelso, a farmhand, gave a deathbed confession; he murdered the Blochmans' son during an argument.

A Type A personality, Ida continued to teach, botanize, lecture, and philanthropize, ascending to administration, becoming a school vice principal and the first woman to sit on the Santa Barbara County Board of Education. The Blochmans quit Santa Maria after oil began seeping into their garden, ruining their flower beds. Union Oil Company installed wells at their Cat Canyon ranch, relieving the couple of ever having to work again. In 1908, husband and wife returned to the San Francisco Bay area. Ida remained busy by joining the suffrage movement, serving as president of the Berkeley Charity Commission, and sitting on the Berkeley Board of Education. Her final botanical project involved investigating the medicinal properties of California native plants. In 1931, Ida cleared her frantic schedule by stepping into the afterlife. Lazar held her memorial services at the Little Chapel of Flowers before burying his beloved alongside Harry in the Jewish section of the Santa Maria Cemetery.

Life without Ida wasn't as sweet, and Lazar found himself gravitating towards spiritualism. Mediums were a breeze to find; newspapers advertised the services of many Bay Area spiritualists, and Lazar likely forked over oil money during his attempts to contact the woman who'd been praised by *The American Naturalist* for writing "pleasantly and instructively" about California wildflowers. There's no evidence that Ida was successfully summoned by these spiritual doctors, but if she was, I hope she made her presence known by suffusing séances with California pitcher sage perfume.

In 1946, a motorist hit Lazar as he crossed a San Francisco street. The day after the accident, death reunited him with Ida and Harry, returning him to Santa Maria. If undertakers pumped the Blochmans with formaldehyde, their remains may be poisoning our valley. If not, as the Jewish tradition precludes embalmment, then the Blochmans are composting, enriching our loam.

Ninety or so years after Ida arrived in the Santa Maria Valley, my father did the same. Like the pistol-packing schoolmarm, he was brought here to teach kids to read. Like the pistol-packing schoolmarm, California native plants fascinate him. Unlike the pistol-packing schoolmarm, my father doesn't collect plant specimens. Instead, he tends an oak forest that I helped him create.

A monster lives there.

That means that a monster lives here too.

A SANTA ANA PEANUT GROWER:
Tells All About How to Plant and Cultivate Goobers.

Santa Maria Times, Saturday, March 14, 1891

Several farmers and gardeners in the Santa Maria Valley tried the raising of peanuts or goobers last season. Some made quite a success of it while others failed. If properly managed there is no need for failure....

GOOBER

If ketchup is a vegetable, then so are books.

    I came to this conclusion after learning the history of paper.

    Much of that history is at one with its subject of inquiry.

History should be kept away from fire.

    Most of it's flammable.

    That's what we get for burdening plants with it.

In Spanish, leaves are hojas.

    In Spanish, hojas are also pages.

    Books are, therefore, word salads.

In Spanish, flor is flower.

    In English, floor is not a flower, but flowers do live in the ground, a floor-like place.

My Mexican grandfather was born on the dirt floor of the jacal that his father built.

Its thatched roof was made of palm fronds.

When you wander a maze, you walk in circles.

You walk in circles when you wander in a daze.

The Spanish word for leaf/page stems from Latin and no, I won't apologize for puns.

Low-hanging literary fruit is a gift.

Folium.

Folio.

Foliage.

Quercus agrifolia, the coastal live oak, is an incomparably seductive tree. A muse. I planted some with my father, but before my dad taught me to read lobed leaves, he introduced me to paper magic.

This began in the womb.

My parents read newspapers and magazines aloud to me while I squirmed *in utero.*

I listened.

I heard that wild things were happening outside of my mother.

An heiress named Patty Hearst had robbed a bank and was going to prison.

The United States of America had elected a peanut farmer as president.

The president of Mexico had ordered a massacre of university students in Tlatelolco.

Educating me about the world that I would soon join ensured that I was an anxious but well-informed fetus.

I was born during a dry year that followed a dry year.

PG&E warned California's farmers. The company threatened rolling blackouts.
    Without electricity, no farmer could run his well.
    Without well water, crops would wither.

Cattle struggled to find anything green to chew.

During earlier droughts, some desperate ranchers had led their cattle to cliffs.

They coaxed them into doing like lemmings.

In California, dry spells come and go, establishing a seasonal rhythm, stretching autumn long, making it last for years.

When the sky withholds rain, we experience wet dreams.

Waterfall fantasies.
    Ice sculptures.
    Lakes that host freshwater mermaids.

My father taught me to read using a children's book that was set at the sea.

To become a proficient reader, a girl must develop her ear.

She must listen for rhyme and rhythm.

The same week that an obstetrician yanked me out of my mother, President Jimmy Carter landed in California. He met with fellow farmers and toured our parched countryside, surveying our water supply and wilting crops.

In the San Joaquin Valley, President Carter visited a citrus and olive farm. With his sleeves rolled up, he strolled the soil, inspecting the drip irrigation system.

Drip.

   Drip.

   Drop.

   Drip.

   Drip.

Drop.

Drip.

Drip.

Drip.

Amniotic fluid.

According to the National Peanut Board, peanuts are a water-efficient crop.

   They drink less than tree nuts.

President Carter climbed a stage and addressed California's farmers.

   He reminded them of his work with peanuts.

   He predicted that a continued drought would likely trigger higher food prices.

   He promised water.

Agua.

Canchalagua.

Chuquiragua.

One may infer rhythm from static experiences.

One may confer rhythm through ecstatic experiences.

Rhythm establishes architecture.

Drip.
Drip.
Drip.

It also enhances predictability.

My dad says that reading requires dialogue, that it's a conversation.

Conversations establish unique rhythms.

Conversations require that all participants think ahead.

A good reader asks herself, "Where is this going?"

Better yet, she asks herself, "Where are *we* going?"

She holds her breath.

Wondering what happens next promotes anticipatory ecstasy.

Did you see the picture of me and my dad? The one where we're sitting on the floral sofa?

It was taken in the living room of our first house, the stucco home that stood across the street from strawberry fields.

A book rests between us.

Its front cover touches my leg. The back touches Dad's.

The book teaches kids about baby animals, going through the unique vocabulary we use to name them.

Tadpoles transform into frogs.

Kits transform into foxes.

Joeys transform into kangaroos.

Cubs transform into bears.

Calves transform into cows.

Cygnets transform into swans.

Fawns transform into deer.

My father's lips move, enunciating words I've never heard.

He points at a platypus.

I laugh.

That's what I'm doing in most of my baby pictures.

Hyena-ing.

I wasn't taught to read with the baby animal book. I was taught to read with a criminal animal book. Its story introduced me to Nat the rat, a rodent who walked on his hind legs and sliced cheese with a saber. Piracy made him rich, and the treasures that Nat amassed through raids lent his career a macho appeal.

This buccaneer became my first literary role model.

Dad read *Nat the Rat* to me until I could recite it with my eyes shut.

One day, when Dad was in the yard watering, I picked up *Nat the Rat*. I sat on my bedroom floor, placed it on my lap, and opened it. My eyes traced the story's letters until the letters formed words and the words coalesced into sentences and these built a maritime world that I was able to enter without my father.

He had made it so that I could now sail the seven seas with thieving rats.

I'm thankful that I learned the term "swashbuckler" before I learned the term "gender role."

The year before Charlotte and I created our girls-only club, I plopped into a circle made up of five classmates seated cross-legged on the playground sand. It was recess and the girls were taking turns answering the same question, "How many kids will you have?"

Everyone was giving elaborate, well-considered answers that followed a spine-tingling pattern.

"One boy and one girl!"

"Four boys and three girls!"

"Two boys and four cats!"

"Two girls and three boys!"

Was becoming a mom inevitable?

I envisioned an avalanche of burping, crying, and spitting babies.

I shuddered. That was *a lot* of bodily fluids.

If I planned on someday growing whiskers and marauding the Atlantic, I couldn't be hampered by parenting.

When my turn came to state how many kids I'd have, I answered, "None."

Eyebrows rose. A jaw or two dropped.

I guess some girls hadn't considered that having zero babies was as valid as having a thousand.

"Why don't you want any?" someone asked.

Weirdo, I thought.

"There's no room for children on a pirate ship," I said.

My classmates and I bickered about this.

While two of them agreed that a pirate ship was no place for an infant, the other two decided that feminism, which they'd learned about from TV talk shows, had changed things. The world was warming up to girls. There had to be room for a mom and her baby on a pirate ship. If Geraldine Ferraro could run for vice president, then of course a lady could breastfeed at sea.

Most nights, at bedtime, Dad would read a book to us. He often reminded us that when a person reads to entertain others, they should do so with emotion. After modeling what that meant, Dad would hand one of us the evening's book and encourage us to mimic him. That was how I learned that it is possible to read with too much emotion.

The aunt who took me to see Judy Garland's house in Lancaster was so into Egyptian history that she gave her Yorkshire terrier a pharaonic name—Khufu. For my eighth birthday, this aunt gave me several books about her favorite subject.

One of these gifts, *Ancient Egyptians*, taught me that it's a plant.

Here's how this lesson unfolded.

I'm hanging out in my room, reading.

I turn to page 6 of *Ancient Egyptians*.

I see a list with the heading "The indispensable papyrus."

The author explains that this tall sedge, which grew in abundance along the Nile, had many purposes. Dried papyrus was used as fuel. Its stalks could be fashioned into boats. Those things are cool but even cooler is that this feather-duster-looking reed was turned into paper.

Was *Ancient Egyptians* also plant-based?

It had to be.

Realizing that my book was a plant, that most books are plants, was delightful and strange.

I wonder what plants think about their role in human communication.

Human history wouldn't exist without them.

Most of it is written all over them.

After reading page 6 of *Ancient Egyptians*, I saw papyrus everywhere.

Toilet paper stuck to my mom's shoe?

Papyrus.

A brown paper lunch bag?

Papyrus.

A piñata being beaten by a blindfolded child?

Papyrus.

A hornet's nest?

Papyrus.

A pizza box?

Papyrus.

A chewing gum wrapper twisting in the breeze?

Papyrus.

What is this page made of?

If its paper, it's probably coniferous.

When we read paper, we find ourselves in a folk song.

Our eyes wander…in the pines…

Paper was once a sacred object, a gift worthy of the gods, a luxury good valuable enough to be used as tribute.

Before Mexico was Mexico, the land had many different names and was occupied by many different nations. Some of these people invented paper. They wove one kind from palm and spun another type from maguey. The most common kind was made using fig or mulberry bark.

In Nahuatl, this bark paper is amatl.

In Mexican mouths, amatl is hispanicized, becoming amate.

In Tenochtitlán, the seat of the Mexica Empire, priests penned books, filling amate with stories of gods, monsters, and heroes. Legal records were kept on amate. Ledgers were amate. Priests wore amate vestments during ceremony. Shamans offered amate to spirits.

Tributaries of the Mexica Empire supplied authorities in Tenochtitlán with 480,000 sheets of amate a year.

Forty villages were dedicated to the production of this good alone.

When Spanish colonists invaded the land that would become Mexico, they torched native libraries and archives. Histories, atlases, and law books were eaten by flame. The Spanish colonial government passed laws prohibiting natives from making or using paper. They imported pale cotton-based sheets which they called European paper. Spanish officials scoffed at its Indigenous counterpart, deriding these brown sheets as papel de tierra.

Earth paper sounds so much prettier than white people paper.

Natives rebelled, producing amate in secret.

Indigenous people living in Mexico still produce amate.

Some ancient amate-producing people lived in western Mexico, in what would become the state of Jalisco.

My dad told me that what we know about these paper producers we know from ancient graves.

Three of my grandparents were born in Jalisco.
        Two are buried in Jalisco's soil.

Arcelia.
Ricardo.

In 1993, a construction crew working near Jalisco's Tequila Volcano* dug into an ancient village. The state contacted archeologists, and they swarmed Huitzilapa, dug more, and discovered an undisturbed shaft tomb, the first of its kind. Until then, archeologists had only been able to inspect shaft tombs emptied by grave robbers.

Guess who owned some of these looted artifacts.

Probably Frida Kahlo.

A lot of art collections are just dead people's stolen stuff.

---

* Doesn't that sound like a volcano that shoots tequila?

Shaft tombs are exactly what they sound like, crypts that one reaches by descending a narrow, vertical tunnel. These entrances may stretch as long as sixty-five feet. Others are as short as ten.

In Huitzilapa, archeologists slid down a tunnel that cut through clay and volcanic rock. In two separate chambers, they found six human skeletons. Five of them may have been family; they shared similar spinal defects. Jade, nacre, earplugs, earrings, metates, slate discs, trumpets, beads, and bowls were heaped around the deceased. Conch shells placed on the loins of one skeleton whispered that he may have been a shaman. Near his skull rested a scrap of amate. Archeologists estimate that it's approximately two thousand years old, making it the oldest bark paper artifact ever found.

It's not weird to give amate to someone who matters.
The traditional first-anniversary gift is paper.

The archeological site by the Tequila Volcano no longer exists.
Bulldozers plowed it so that farmers could plant more agave.
Huitzilapa's ruins were ruined to make way for a ruinous liquor.
Tequila.

Prayer cards.
Letters.
Pictures.
Pan dulce wrapped in napkins.
Children's drawings.

In my family, we continue to bury our dead with paper.

I remember a book that wore a brittle and yellowing jacket made from paper-turned-parchment. Water had ruined it, staining it with brownish blobs that looked vaguely floral. Its edges flaked, crumbling when stroked.

"Once when I was six years old, I saw a magnificent picture in a book called *True Stories from Nature*, about the primeval forest."

Dad had begun reading to us.

He turned *The Little Prince* around so that we could see the picture: A boa constrictor swallowing an animal.

The story's narrator sketches his own version, but when he shows his drawing to grown-ups, they mistake it for a hat. Disgusted by their lack of imagination, the narrator distances himself from adults. When he inevitably grows up, he becomes a pilot. Like Dorothy in *The Wizard of Oz*, he crashes. His plane goes down in the Sahara, where he makes the acquaintance of the little prince.

I inferred that my dad was fond of the pilot's story because of the boa constrictor.

Dad loves snakes.

I liked *The Little Prince* because the little prince looked like Charlotte. My best friend had the same yellow hair and the same narrow nose.

I wondered if the little prince was part Cherokee.

Charlotte bragged that she was part Cherokee princess.

Dad told me she wasn't.

The little prince asks the pilot to draw him a sheep.

He obliges.

Lambs become sheep.

Boys become men.

Fig trees become paper.

Paper becomes sacred.

The little prince lives on a faraway planet, Asteroid B-612.
He shares his home with a few baobab trees and a rose.
She talks a lot.

Baobabs look like upside down trees.
Bats pollinate them at night.

The oldest living baobab is around the same age as the oldest amate.

The Spanish word for leaf is derived from Latin.

The Spanish word for page is derived from Latin.

They're the same word.

Hoja.
Hoja.
Ojalá.

Hoja.
Hoja.
Ojalá.

MURDER MOST FOUL:
A Man Murdered Near Cholame and His Body Cremated.

Santa Maria Times, Saturday, August 17, 1895

On arriving there they found the body in a burning brush heap, which had been built alongside a fallen oak tree, with both legs entirely consumed and the face burnt to a crisp....

BURBUJA

Water boils in a pot on my stove.

I sit at the dining room table.

I've moved some plants out of my way to create a workspace.

Assembled before me are a pair of scissors, a freshly sharpened No 2. pencil, and a brown paper grocery bag.

I loop my fingers through the scissors' smooth handles and reach for the paper.

Snip.

Snip.

Snip.

I place the strip on the table. Its shape reminds me of a cadaver.

A girl can dream....

I run my fingers across the pulpy texture, smoothing wrinkles.

Next, I pick up the pencil and raise it to my nostrils.

I inhale. Close my eyes.

Pine...

I drag the graphite across the strip of paper, spelling the name of the marijuana prince.

When I'm done, I set down my pencil and carry my effigy to the stove.

Feet first: that's how I introduce him into the boiling water.

I take my time submerging him, toying with him.

Once I let go, the elements attack.

He twists this way and that, this way and that.

His head slams against the side of the pot.

Bang. Bang. Bang.

(A crow caws in the alley. She's cheering me on!)

To escape further injury, the marijuana prince dives to the bottom of the pot. Then, he bobs back up to the surface, as if gasping for air.

I grab my wooden spoon and beat him down.

In Spanish, bubble is burbuja.

In Spanish, witch is bruja.

In Oz, witches travel by bubble.

A bruja in a burbuja.

B u R b U J A

The water has evaporated.

The marijuana prince catches fire, twisting, curling, burning at the bottom of my pot.

He turns to ash.

I turn off the stove, carry the pot outside, and walk to the end of my street, where one road crosses another.

I dispose of his remains there, and as I take the first steps back home, I'm careful not to look over my shoulder.

I ignore what's left of him.

Dirt.

HIGH SCHOOL NOTES:
A Number of Interesting Items from the Temple of Learning.

Santa Maria Times, Saturday, March 7, 1896

On Friday of last week while the recitation in geometry was in progress, Harold Philbrick heard an unusual commotion in the stove. Upon investigation it proved to be a large handsome owl. It must have come down through the chimney and stove pipe, and that could be accomplished only by some pretty tight squeezing. After the school had been given an opportunity to inspect him he was given his liberty....

CANTICLE OF
THE CREATURES

In Zacoalco de Torres, during the month of the dead, the Confraternity of the Moors leads an impassioned celebration. This Catholic mutual aid society spends days honoring the town's spiritual guardian, Saint Francis of Assisi.

Pope Gregory IX canonized Francis in 1228, just two short years after his death from malaria. A stone sarcophagus received his sanctified remains.

A poet, Francis wrote *Canticle of the Creatures* one year before his death. In this hymn, he addresses the sun, the moon, and the heavens as family. He also addresses Death as kin, an inescapable relative.

Francis famously preached to nonhumans. He once delivered a sermon to a field of curious birds. Before he left, he blessed his winged parishioners.

Friar Thomas of Celano authored three Franciscan hagiographies. In *The Remembrance of the Desire of a Soul*, he describes Francis' monastic garden: "He commands the gardener to leave the edges of the garden undug so that in their season the greenness of the grass and the beauty of the flowers may proclaim the beauty of the Father of all. It is designated that within the garden there be a smaller garden for aromatic and flowering plants so that those who see them may be diverted by the memory of the eternal sweetness."

This garden is probably a literary device.

A concrete statue of Francis sunbathes on my parents' back patio.
    He wears Snow White's favorite accessory.

A bird.

In 1550, Franciscan friars brought Jesus to the Province of Avalos.

Indigenous converts built the padres a convent on land that would become Zacoalco de Torres.

Thirty-seven years after the convent's founding, Alonso Ponce, a visiting friar, wrote that "the village of Tzacoalco is big and populated by Indians...almost all of them understand and speak Nahuatl..."

Xochitl means flower in Nahuatl.

Malinalxochitl means creeping flower in Nahuatl.

Clematis creeps.
Honeysuckle creeps.
Morning glory creeps.

Malinalxochitl, a great sorceress who angered the Mexica gods by acquiring her powers illicitly, destroys those who cross her.

Several creatures do her bidding.
The snake.
The scorpion.
The centipede.
The spider.

Francis, patron saint of animals, is rarely shown ministering to insects or arachnids.

The butterfly *Neonympha mitchellii francisci* is named after the saint. This insect is endangered. She faces extinction and ranks as one of the rarest butterflies in the world.

In Zacoalco, a bordered patch butterfly approaches a blossoming guamúchil. She unfurls her proboscis and sucks. Drinks.

Speaking of vampiric creatures, my mother's mother told me the story of the tlahuelpuchi.

She, too, has a proboscis.

The tlahuelpuchi is a woman by day, a turkey by night.

In her Thanksgiving form, she stalks villages, looking for newborns.

When she smells one, she approaches. If the house has no window large enough for a turkey to squeeze through, the tlahuelpuchi shrinks, turning into a mosquito. At the infant's bedside, she returns to poultry. From her beak unfurls a proboscis. She plunges it into the infant.

Sips.

Gobble gobble.

Chirimías squeal.
  Drummers tap tap tap.
  Trumpets wail.
  Tico toco tocoto.
  Tico toco tocoto.
  Clad in maroon capes, four masked escorts balance bulbous flower-studded crowns on their heads. They accompany the statue of Saint Francis through the streets of Zacoalco, guarding him. When the entourage arrives at the house of the family chosen to host him, they set the statue on the home altar, a wooden table decorated with guachúmil branches and roses.

Born in nearby Techaluta in 1900, José Ramirez Flores spent his childhood in Zacoalco. In 1960, he published *Indigenous Matrimony in Zacoalco*, a monograph that describes the native community's nuptial customs. The book also hints at another custom.

Hechicería.

In Zacoalco, certain bird sounds signal the presence of a witch.

Tico toco tocoto.
Tico toco tocoto.

Beware the nocturnal music sung by owls.

Jú.
Jú.
Jú.

Should you fall ill for no discernible reason, consider your enemies.

Who have you recently insulted?

In Zacoalco, witches make rag dolls representing those who have offended them. The women stab them with cactus thorns, beating the dolls until the offender bleeds. Once they've sated their desire for revenge, the witches bury these dolls.

The groove-billed ani, an inky black member of the cuckoo family, has terrorized Zacoalco for hundreds of years. Some call her the ticuz. Slightly larger than a grackle, this bird has a large, curved beak whose weight might be the reason for her clumsiness. While this dopey creature may seem harmless, the ticuz might as well fly with a scythe. She takes souls.

A man whose long-suffering wife serves him a dish made with the meat of this bird will fall into a stupor from which he'll never recover.

"Praised be You, my Lord, through our Sister Bodily Death, from whom no one living can escape."

Who?
Who?
Who?

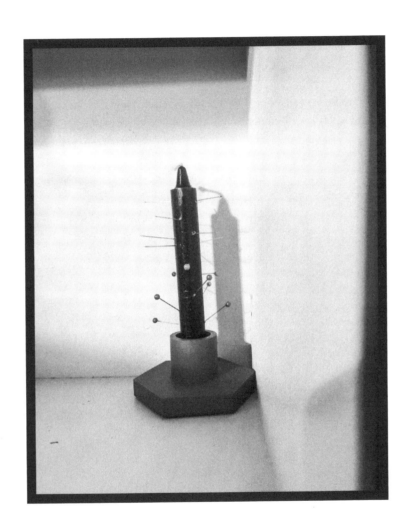

"On September 30, 1856, in the village of San Cristóbal, Jalisco, Mexico, the native population was summoned by indigenous governor Lugardo Onofre of Zacoalco de Torres. Citizens were urged to convoke town halls and during these meetings, a plan to exact justice was developed by the indigenous people of Zacoalco. Armed forces have been assembled for the sole and exclusive purpose of ending the bloody conflict over property and ensuring the return of lands usurped by haciendas."

—A Proclamation from San Cristóbal and Zacoalco de Torres

OUR WILDFLOWERS:
Tarweed and Other Roadside Pests Get an Airing.

Santa Maria Times, Saturday, October 8, 1892

Tarweed is so common hereabout that it is impugning your intelligence to describe it....

PETRIFIED

The emergence of the hungry clouds from the hills of Rancho Suey coincided with the death of Wodziwob, originator of the Ghost Dance. Years prior, this Northern Paiute had prophesied that a locomotive filled with his nation's dead would be arriving from the east. He spoke of his visions throughout pinenut country, and to hasten the resurrection, Indians organized Round Dance ceremonies that lasted days. Exhausted participants would collapse onto wildflower-carpeted meadows and slip into trances, coming face to face with talkative ghosts. Wodziwob's message spread to the Owens Valley and beyond, and in some parts of this newly minted state, Indians spent the entire summer dancing.

While Rancho Suey's hungry clouds went unforeseen by Wodziwob, Indian technology could've prevented them from forming in the first place. California needed to be burned, but the American pioneers who now controlled the land refused to perform fire duties. Instead, they let weeds grow and grow and grow, allowing them to become a matted and tangled carpet that a few carefully placed embers could've easily taken care of. Cattlemen wanted this dense vegetation for their livestock. They didn't anticipate what else they were feeding.

An Old Testament menace.

In *The Natural Wealth of California*, chronicler Titus Fey Cronise notes that the region's many uninvited visitors left records attesting to the rich cornucopia which they invaded. These explorers marveled at elk, deer, antelope, rabbit, and quail grazing in verdant valleys and plains. They stumbled upon rivers and lakes that swarmed with duck, geese, turtle, salmon, and trout, their beds and banks encrusted with mussel, clam, and other mollusks. They gawked in disbelief at how many seals and otters crowded the shores and at how generously woodlands and forests rained berries, nuts and seeds.

Dazzled by their edible surroundings, the Europeans misinterpreted what they saw. Native technology had crafted an expansive network of gardens that supplied California Indians with everything they could ever need. Nevertheless, racism prevented Spanish settlers from recognizing that Indians were scientists, engineers, and land stewards. When the Spanish Crown laid claim to native lands, white officials classified Alta California's Indigenous peoples as "gente sin razón," a euphuism for savages.

Chumash women served as their nation's fire technicians, and the territory that they managed stretched from Malibu to Paso Robles. For millennia, the burns orchestrated by these matriarchs had generated rich plant and animal diversity. By declaring that neither "Indians nor Gentiles" could wield flame, the Spanish colonial government disrupted age-old strategies. In 1793, Governor José Joaquín de Arrillaga ordered that anyone caught setting fire to fields or pastures would be severely punished for their "childishness." His ban reframed environmental stewardship as pyromania, and the new policy made it that much harder for Indians to be Indians.

That was the point.

Starving Indians flocked to the Franciscan missions dotting California's coast. Five of these death traps were erected on the soil where I was born, Chumash land. After receiving the holy rite of baptism, Indians became prisoners; Spanish law prohibited them from leaving mission grounds without permission. Forced to work in the padres' vineyards, neophytes planted, pruned, fertilized, harvested, and crushed *Vitis vinifera*, a grape originally from Castilla La Mancha that was used to make sacramental and table wine. Indians toiled from six in the morning until sunset and were prohibited from imbibing the fruits of their labor. No cognac, rum, or aguardiente, only a splash of Jesus' blood on Sundays and no seconds.

Flogging was a common punishment for perceived insolence, idleness, or drunkenness. Some mission runaways who were recaptured were marked by branding irons and then lashed. One eyewitness watched as soldiers found an Indian chief who'd deserted the missions. Spaniards marched him into an open field where a dead calf had begun to rot. After skinning the animal, the soldiers wrapped the chief in the hide and sewed him into it, suffocating him with the improvised sarcophagus. The assassins left the chief's remains tied to a stake, a warning.

In 1821, the Spanish Empire ceded Alta California to the newly constituted Mexican Empire. This regime change further hurt the Chumash. Now forced to work for the Mexican army, Indians received IOUs in lieu of wages. Mexican officials who'd once assured natives that their lands would be returned broke their promises. Chumash watched as Mexican politicians, ranchers, and soldiers received tracts of land that'd been theirs. The continued depredation inspired rage. In 1823, natives from three different missions—La Purísima, Santa Inés, and Santa Barbara—plotted.

The rebels decided to strike on February 22, 1824. A beating moved the attack up one day early. A Mexican soldier at Mission Santa Inés took offense when a Purisimeño Chumash who'd come to visit an imprisoned relative reminded him that, until recently, the missions had been under Spanish dominion. The soldier brutalized the visitor, and news of the Mexican assault travelled fast, igniting a response. Rebels torched Mission Santa Inés until most of its buildings were engulfed in the warmest of colors.

Archers set out to find Father Francisco Xavier de la Concepción Uría, a priest from Pamplona notorious for whacking Chumash kids on the head with a stick. The padre had designed Mission Santa Inés, and he was napping when a servant woke him and warned him about the armed Indians assembled outside his room. Unfortunately, Uría managed to grab his musket, take aim, and fire. Fortunately, some Chumash escaped to the San Joaquin Valley, where Yokuts sheltered them.

During the brief period that Alta California was Mexican, a woman became one of the province's wealthiest landowners. In 1826, Maria Ramona la Luz Carrillo married José Antonio Romualdo Pacheco, a doomed engineering officer. He was either shot by pistol or skewered by lance at the Battle of

Cahuenga Pass. Regardless of what tore the fatal hole, Doña Pacheco became a widow. In 1837, she received a consolation prize. Governor Juan Bautista Valentín Alvarado y Vallejo granted her 48,800 acres of her natal province.

Rancho Suey, which spanned the Santa Maria and Cuyama rivers, served as the Widow Pacheco's dowry. This wealth accentuated her decaying beauty, and it attracted sea captain "Juan" Wilson, a Scottish merchant who'd sailed the Pacific on the *Ayacucho*, a three-hundred-ton brig built in Guayaquil, Ecuador. To ready himself for marriage, Captain Wilson converted to Catholicism. By saying "I do," he became a Mexican citizen. This religious, and political, metamorphosis allowed him to take his wife's lands and other ranchos. Wilson's tracts sustained around fifteen thousand head of cattle and countless wild but scrawny horses.

When Captain Wilson died, drought struck. Livestock starved. Cows laid down, shut their eyes, and trotted to heaven. Vaqueros rode from carcass to carcass, skinning, removing hides quickly.

Shadows with wide wingspans circled the desiccated beef.

Vultures.

The hungry clouds of locusts emerged from the rocky crevices of Rancho Suey once their wings were strong enough for flight. Swarming, they converged, forming what almost seemed to be billows of smoke that eclipsed Santa Maria's sun, moon, and clouds. Hawks, falcons, and eagles hid. The sky was too busy. Landlocked birds, mostly turkey, quail, and chicken, rejoiced, lunching on the millions of locusts chewing their way through the valley. In the weeks following the bug invasion, plump hens laid a surplus of eggs that no pioneer woman wanted to poach. Their shells housed bad omens. Instead of yellow, their yolks bled red.

Perhaps it was the tarweed that had lured and fattened these late-nineteenth-century bugs. This herb is kin to California sagebrush and California sunflower, members of the plant family *Asteraceae*. Poet Margaret S. Cobb calls tarweed the "sweet vagrant of the valley," and its comet-like rosettes bloom in May, withering in August. Humans, bugs, birds, chipmunks, and rabbits have all developed a taste for this plant, and Rancho Suey, Suey Crossing, and Suey Road all take their names from swey, a Chumash word for tarweed.

Swey was the name of a Chumash village that once bustled east of Santa Maria, but I didn't know that it had influenced the name of our street.

I thought it was called Suey Road because that's what the branches of the sycamore trees lining it did when the wind blew.

The wind blew a lot.

California blackberries grew along our Suey house's backyard fence. I crawled into their dark green brambles and became a locust. Farmers planted strawberry fields across the street, too far away for me to crawl to. Up and down the road, tarweed sprouted. Its funk mingled with the aroma of ripe berries and the spicy scents wafting through the valley from a sugar refinery that is no longer with us.

When I was three or four, we moved a few blocks away from the sycamore trees to a street with a gem of a name, Garnet Way. Our home occupied a large corner lot, and it was here where I began harvesting rocks. My great-grandmother had also harvested rocks, and she understood that spirits lived in them, that they had souls. When she'd overhear that her grandkids were going foraging in the Mexican countryside, she'd assign them geologic errands.

"Bring me back some rocks."

"What kind?"

"The special kind."

"How will we know they're special?"

"You'll know. The rocks will tell you."

My great-grandmother displayed her beloveds, scattering her rocks in the tropical garden that sprouted from her home's floor.

My dad inherited his grandmother's petrofilia.

I inherited his.

The hills that the locusts emerged from were rocky, likely filled with stones that would've made my mouth water. I usually rock harvested close to home. Instead of a lawn, the Garnet house had gravel- and rock-filled yards, like

Pebble Beach. With last year's Easter basket in hand, I stepped carefully, gathering treasure. When I fell and skinned my knees, I got up, ignored my bleeding, and continued the harvest. I did the same at the vacant lot down the road. Rock harvesting there was slightly more exciting. Ornery rattlesnakes could be found sunbathing behind abandoned refrigerators. So could boys with BB guns.

My dad's rocks made mine look amateurish. The Garnet house had a small den where we kept the TV and most of our books, including field guides for prospecting, treasure hunting, and rock, gem, and mineral identification. My hamster lived in a cage by the den's sliding glass door which Mom covered in dinosaur decals. These extinct animals were there to prevent pedestrians from walking into the door. My brother tended to do that when I cleaned it too well.

Dad displayed some of his rocks on the den's redbrick fireplace. One was a slab of petrified wood that Dad said had come from a petrified forest where all the trees had turned to stone. I'd seen petrification happen in movies. The same channel that aired *The Wizard of Oz* also broadcast *Clash of the Titans*, and as a family we sat on our couch, watching Perseus decapitate Medusa and then save her head in a bag. Later, Perseus pulls it out and dangles it by its snake hair to turn enemies into stone.

Had Medusa visited the forest where the tree on our fireplace had once cast shade?

If so, had the tree seen Medusa?

Could trees see?

Could trees hear?

Did they have imaginations?

The possibilities were troubling and exciting.

The fireplace slab wasn't our only piece of petrified wood, but it was our largest. It felt cool to the touch, and it confused. How could something simultaneously feel like stone *and* wood? My fingertips rubbed trunk fiber and my eyes saw lumber, but at the same time, I saw and felt rock. The only thing I fondled more than that former tree was my hamster. By the time we left the Garnet house for the house on the hill, the petrified slab had grown greasy. My nose-picking fingers had lightly coated it with filth.

Dad had more cool stuff. On the fireplace mantle rested a very old tooth which might have once belonged to a horse. There were trilobite and fish fossils and a conch shell and dried starfish that stank like yesterday's scrod. I wondered if that's what Dad's octopuses had smelled like. When he and his brother Henry were kids, they found these cephalopods along with a bunch of sea spiders at the tidepools in Corona del Mar. They brought them back home, to Norwalk, where the animals lived in aquariums at the back of the garage, by the boxes where my grandmother stashed copies of *True Detective*.

My father was born in Miami, Florida, but mostly grew up in Mexico and California. He hated being indoors and so he spent a lot of his childhood on his bicycle, pedaling out of Norwalk and into the wilds of Orange County. Henry went with him. They fancied themselves paleontologists and brought shovels and buckets on their excursions.

"A well-trained lizard hunter knows how to read the natural world," Dad told my brother, sister, and me when teaching us how to scout for reptiles in our backyard. Dad told us that across the street from his house in Norwalk, he and Henry staked out places attractive to reptiles, sunbaked wooden boards abandoned in the brome. The brothers crept up on these planks, flipped them, and grabbed alligator lizards by their tails, dropping them into potato sacks. These well-camouflaged creatures bit. They drew blood.

Catching gopher snakes required a different technique. We watched Dad tiptoe toward these reptiles and grab them behind the head, never by the tail. "They're like humans!" Dad called out as he dangled an angry gopher snake a few feet away from himself. "When they panic, they make caca!"

Dad and Henry pedaled out to La Mirada and Los Coyotes. Men on motorcycles watched them, nodding with approval at the little adventurers. The foothills were scrubby and thick with nopales whose fruit my New-Jersey-bred grandfather had developed a taste for. Grandpa Peter carried a pocketknife and would gently cut prickly pears loose, letting them fall to the earth. Using a twig, he taught his kids to roll the fruit back and forth, letting the soil de-thorn it. Cactus apples and other foraged foods fueled his kids' fossil hunts.

The brothers found pectens and other ancient sea creatures that proved that California had once been ocean floor. They dug up whale parts and the remains of early horses. Once Henry learned to drive, they took Grandpa's car out to the boonies and returned with cardboard boxes filled with stones that once had a pulse. They donated one of their finds to the Natural History Museum. To honor Henry's generosity, curators invited him to a reception. There, he received a certificate of appreciation for his gift, a section of the pelvic region of a giant ground sloth.

–

CURRENT NEWS

Santa Maria Times, Saturday January 12, 1901

An unusual vocation has been adopted by Professor von Keith of Los Angeles, who has been in Kern County for some months, attracted by the variety of mineral and fossil remains to be found out there. His latest labor has been the gathering of fish bones and skins from the bed of Buena Vista Lake....

POLISH THINGS

Have you heard of the Leshy? He's why my dad stayed safe playing outside.

Leshy is short for leśny duch, Polish forest spirit, though he's really more of a forest protector.

The Leshy changes shape according to whim. This gift complicates identifying him. He might appear to a greedy hunter as an ogre with a flowing beard of lichen and an ankle-length coat made of swishing beech leaves. A young woman foraging for mushrooms might glimpse him in the form of a one-eyed sprite lounging atop a toadstool. To a greedy lumberjack, the Leshy might manifest as sound. Should he reveal himself as laughter that comes at you from the forest's every direction, run.

Hurry...

A hungry Leshy is more dangerous than one who's well-fed. To pacify him, prepare a basket. Line it with bark cloth. Fill it with offerings. Bring the basket to the forest and place it at the foot of what feels like the oldest tree. Hardboiled eggs, fresh bread, honey, and a deck of playing cards should keep him happily occupied.

The Leshy has a soft spot for children in danger.
        He draws them outdoors and into the forest.

The forest is a place of ambiguity.
        It can feed us. It can ruin us.

My girl, my girl, don't lie to me,

                        Tell me where did you sleep last night?
            In the pines, in the pines, where the sun never shines,
                        And I shivered the whole night through...

What kind of weather did your childhood home have? Was it mild or stormy?

My father's childhood homes were tempestuous.
        Injury was guaranteed.

My father's mother used an assortment of implements to "discipline" her children. She purchased these tools at a saddlery. They were intended for use on horses.

Bruise.
Lacerate.
Flay.

That's what my grandmother did to her kids.

I would bet money that someone treated Grandma like livestock when she was a little girl.

Someone taught her that kids are animals and that animals are objects.

That person was probably her dad.

Grandma went by her middle name, Hope. She was born in Guadalajara, Mexico, on April 27, 1926.

Queen Elizabeth II was born in London, England on April 21, 1926.

During Hope's childhood, true-crime journalism became Mexico's most popular form of print entertainment.

Young Hope skimmed bloody Mexican tabloids and comic books, learning about the many ways that humans torture one another.

In the city of Guadalajara, a municipal decree prohibited anyone who wasn't a licensed pharmacist from harvesting henbane, belladonna, yellow oleander, hemlock, coral tree, and angel's trumpet. Any one of these plants could be turned into a tea powerful enough to free a wife from a "difficult" marriage.

When she was seventeen, Hope married Peter, a visiting gringo.

A friend of my mother's once saw my grandparents' wedding portrait and gasped. She mistook Hope for me and freaked out. Why had I been taken as some old gringo's child bride?

I know little about the circumstances of my Grandpa Peter's birth. I know that his mother, Maria Pikiołek, worked as a housekeeper for the Goldbaums, a Jewish family that bought her headstone. I know that she died of tuberculosis on February 23, 1917, at age twenty-five. I know that eight-year-old Peter attended his mother's funeral. I know that Peter's aunt handed him two pennies when the wake was over and with them jingling in his pocket, he skipped to the store and paid for a few pieces of hard candy. I know that when Peter arrived at his aunt's house, she asked, "Where are the pennies I gave you?" I know that he answered honestly, and I hate what she did.

She smacked him and said, "Those were the pennies that we used to cover your mother's eyes! You weren't supposed to spend them, idiot!"

When Dad repeats that story, I feel sorry for Grandpa. He was just trying to sweeten a hard day.

During the second world war, the U.S. Army drafted Peter. He and Hope took trains from Jalisco to Florida. In this peninsula packed with orange groves, Peter sat at a desk, hunched over files, squinting, ruining his eyes. He worked as a censor, and I imagine him poring over documents, his sleeves rolled up, a marker with a fat felt tip in his grip as he blacks out word after word after word, a top-secret erasure poet.

Hope and Peter took up residence in a rented trailer that teetered on stilts, and they probably conceived my dad, who they nicknamed Butch, around the time that herpetologist Bill Haast broke ground on his Miami Serpentarium. A concrete stone cobra towered outside of this snake park's entrance on South Dixie Highway. Tourists flocked to Haast's zoo, where he gained a reputation as a master reptile handler. Donning a white lab coat, Haast performed acts of herpetological daredevilry, grabbing reptiles with his bare hands and milking them for venom which he later injected into himself. According to his wife, Nancy, Haast was a superman; he survived 172 bites. Haast believed that reptile venom held the key to human longevity, and his death at age one hundred suggests that the centenarian might've been onto something.

Goodbye, Florida, land of cobras and oranges and trailers that hop on stilts...

Hope and Peter returned to Guadalajara. With two sons and a daughter, they were now a family of five.

In Mexico, Butch and Henry hunted for stones for their grandmother's rock collection. They also played by Mercado San Juan de Díos, a place where you could buy anything, even a squirrel on a flimsy leash.

Butch and Henry walked their squirrel to their grandmother's. She ordered them to cage him. They did but the squirrel slipped through the wires and escaped out the kitchen window.

His bushy tail waved bye.

The squirrel made his home beneath my great-grandmother's. Against her will, she fed him.

My great-grandmother placed tortillas on the window ledge, letting the sun suck the moisture from them.

The squirrel smelled this food and emerged, climbing to the window. He snatched the hardening tortillas, dragging them back to his lair, where he shredded them, making his own chilaquiles.

In 1952, Hope and Peter left Mexico again, travelling to California by train.

Butch and Henry missed their Mexican squirrel, but their new neighborhood in Norwalk had new squirrels and lots of alligator lizards. In nearby Buena Park, at the California Alligator Farm, children rode alligators. The reptiles wore saddles and swam through ponds with little girls and little boys strapped to their carnivorous backs. Occasionally, the ponds flooded, and alligators went missing.

So did squirrels.

Hope sat on the living room couch, skimming gruesome tabloids. Peter's snoring rattled the bedroom door. He was napping, preparing for the night shift at the airplane factory. Butch and Henry were miles away, wandering southern California's nopal forests, looking for places to dig.

The Leshy had summoned them.

Protector of forests, and children, he watched over the brothers while they played. He whispered into their ears, telling them where to take their shovels, murmuring about fossils. By luring them into the hills, he drew the boys far from Hope and her weapons. Yes, there were rattlesnakes and bobcats and mountain lions and bears and questionable flowers out there, but chaparral was safer than home. Rattlesnakes issue warnings. Hope did not.

Though Hope was Mexican, I think of her cruelty in Slavic terms. She was Butch's Baba Yaga.

Many of the Mexicans in my family are challenged by the word Butch.
    They call my father Bush.
    In Spanish, bush is arbusto.

A witch who lives deep in the woods in a hut that hops on two massive chicken legs, Baba Yaga eats children. A resourceful witch, she saves their bones, using them to cobble the skeletal fence that surrounds her travelling hut.

My Polish ancestors lived in a village. Gorlice.

Thistles, daisies, chamomile, and yarrow are some of the flowers that bees pollinate in Gorlice.

The Polish word for honey is similar to the Spanish word for honey.

Miód.

Miel.

Ja nie mówię po polsku is the only sentence that I can say in Polish. Ja nie mówię po polsku means I don't speak Polish. Saying ja nie mówię po polsku to Poles has gotten me in trouble. Polish people perk up when they hear me say that I can't speak Polish in Polish and so they begin speaking to me in more Polish, showering me in their language.

Ja nie mówię po polsku.

I've never been to Poland.

I've never left North America.

There's plenty to see and do right here.

Everything that I know about Poland I've learned from family, books, photographs, and these Poles that I met in univeristy who got me drunk and tried to teach me to dance the polonaise.

I know that Paweł, my Polish great-grandfather, built his house himself. I know that he kept bees.

In Poland, amber is a big deal. So are bees.

Beekeepers once managed Polish forests filled with tree hives. These are made when bees are kept in hollows chopped into old pines with thick trunks. Other hive-conducive trees include fir, elm, linden, and spruce. Oak, too.

Beekeepers once honored Polish kings with wax, lumber, honey, and pine marten pelts. In return, beekeepers received unique privileges. They could collect lumber. They could hunt. They could gather acorns. They could punish those who hurt or killed their bees.

A seventeenth-century Polish edict states that "anyone who willfully takes bees belonging to others, or unlawfully deprives them of their honey, shall be condemned to death on the gallows."

More macabre punishments also existed.

"Whosoever destroys an entire colony of bees, no matter whether they belong to himself or to anybody else, shall be handed over to the public executioner, who shall take his entrails, and wind them round the tree in which the bees were willfully destroyed, and shall afterwards hang him on the same trees."

Picture the surviving Polish bees, who are mourning their slain ancestors, attending one of these tree hangings, relieved that revenge won't require them to sacrifice their stingers.

With the honey that his bees gave him, Paweł brewed mead.

Mead is produced by fermenting must, which is honey diluted with water. Adding fruits, herbs, and spices during or after the fermentation process enriches mead's flavor.

A wooden cup brimming with mead would make a good offering to the Leshy.

He protects pine forest, oak forest, birch forest, saguaro forest, all forest.

He protects bees and acorns and mushrooms and berries and birds and prickly pears and bruised children.

The Leshy and Baba Yaga came to the Americas aboard a ship that crossed the Atlantic, delivering Poles to New York City.

When people leave one continent to settle in another, they bring clothes, microbes, holy books, seeds, recipes, toys, knives, forks, spoons, and blankets. They also bring ghosts, monsters, demons, gods, spirits, hope, confusion, and hidden jars of honey.

TOURISTS SEEK CHANCE TO STARE AT FILM STARS

Santa Maria Times, Friday, March 13, 1925

More than a million tourists come to California annually, and the chief lure for the sightseers is not the ocean, the orange groves, the old Spanish missions, the sunken gardens, or Chinatown. It is Hollywood—dreamland of film fans....

ANAHEIM

A freeway is always being built somewhere in California and these transit projects benefit keen fossil hunters. Butch and Henry pedaled to one such site to find diatomaceous earth heavily disturbed. With spoons and toothbrushes, they chipped away at the limestone, dislodging a chunk.

Oak...

The outline of a fossilized leaf!

This leaf belonged to a tree that lived eons before the ancient trees that Peter introduced his kids to during rare summer vacations. One June, the Douglas Aircraft machinist drove his family north, to Yosemite National Park. There, they met the General Sherman, a sequoia named after the officer who famously ordered Union forces to burn down Atlanta during the Civil War. Before the tree was promoted to officer, he was called Karl Marx. That earlier name had been given to him in 1884, when a band of socialist loggers, the Kaweah colonists, surveyed the area, hoping to establish a utopia. In 1891, U.S. soldiers kicked the hippie colonists out of the park. The General's inclination toward communism went with them.

Peter also took his kids to meet trees in Sequoia National Park. They drove there in the perfect car, a woody wagon, and the family posed for a souvenir photo while motoring through the Tunnel Log, a two-thousand-year-old sequoia that had fallen and been repurposed as a tourist trap. Mostly, Peter took his kids to the drive-in. There, they could eat homemade popcorn, watch a double feature, pass out, and snore. When Peter was extremely broke, he chaperoned his kids on day trips to Buena Park, letting them loose in Knott's Berry Farm, a Wild-West-inspired theme park famous for its chicken dinners and boysenberry pie. Knott's had no admission fee and that made Peter a repeat non-customer.

On sunny afternoons, Peter took his wife and kids for spins in the country, and in the 1950s, Orange County still had lots of country. Early one evening, when the family was returning from a drive, Butch smelled death. The sun had freshly set, but the stars were missing. Smoke blotted their shine. To the north, south, east, and west stood tall roadside pyramids, funeral pyres. Peter slowed so that everyone could safely rubberneck. Parents and kids craned their heads out the woodie wagon's windows, trying to figure out what was being barbecued.

Orange trees.

Pyramids made of stacked and butchered orange trees stretched to the horizon.

A mass citrus-cide.

Juicy.

Ripe.

Tangy.

Death.

The cremation was as fiery as California's state flower.

"Sir, what are they going to build here?" Peter shouted to a guard posted at a fence.

"Disneyland!"

The guard strolled to the driver's side window and handed Peter a job application.

"Thank you."

Peter placed it in the glovebox.

The application was lost.
Like you.

RESTORATION OF PURISIMA TO CONTINUE

Santa Maria Times, Tuesday, November 28, 1939

Work at La Purisima is being done by the National Park Service CCC camp and the project is about two-thirds completed. It is the only undertaking of its kind in the state. When complete it will give the visitor a picture of mission life as it appeared in the mission period....

NICAN TLAMI TOTLATOTZIN

My father wasn't big on fun day trips. Instead, he was into educational outings. We always had to be learning, we could never do anything mindless, and one of the places where he took us, and scared us, was Mission La Purísima. Once a Catholic labor camp, the site had been transformed into an interactive museum, a place where schoolchildren went to experience, and reenact, a decaffeinated version of California's past.

The drive from Santa Maria to La Purísima was lovely.
    Sculptural manzanita twisted along hillsides.
    Deer grazed in the fog.
    Once we passed Vandenberg Air Force Base, flower fields.
    Nibbling at Lompoc's flower fields, rabbits.

Tuxti...

Depressed livestock grazed just beyond La Purísima's nearly empty parking lot.

As we trudged toward the mission's campanile and campo santo, I sniffed at the air.

Hay. Horse shit. Mud.

"Be respectful," Dad warned my brother, sister, and me. "A lot of people were killed here. See the cemetery?"

The three of us nodded and chorused, "Yes."

The campo santo was tiny.

"That cemetery isn't big enough to hold all the Chumash who died here. This whole place is a grave."

Dad's words transformed La Purísima.

Its adobe buildings became a series of haunted houses.

I felt sad for the ghosts.

I wished I could help them leave.

Franciscans founded Misión La Purísima Concepcion to control the Indians of the Santa Barbara Channel Islands. They first built La Purisima on Algascupi, a Chumash village, but it collapsed. Instead of heeding this omen, the padres rebuilt, and an earthquake took this second attempt, flattening it. The third time, they rebuilt at Amúu. This iteration also fell into ruin, but once the Great Depression struck, the California Conservation Corps put men to work restoring the mission grounds, turning the death trap into a state-run colonial theme park.

Historical markers appear throughout the mission grounds.

Stories are printed on them.

Dates are printed on them.

In 1824, the Indians at Santa Inés, La Purísima, and Santa Barbara rebelled.

A lot of what we know about the uprising comes from María Solares.

María Ysidora del Refugio Solares came into this world shortly before the horrors of the California Gold Rush. Of the eleven kids born to her parents, she was the only one to make it past infancy. Brigida, her mother, was Yokut from Kern Lake. Benventura, her father, came from the second-largest Chumash community in Santa Inés, Kalawasaq.

Solares consulted with ethnologist J.P. Harrington to preserve the Samala Chumash language. She also worked with him to document Chumash history, story, and other word-based artforms.

Solares told Harrington about death at La Purísima.

The 1824 uprising began when an Indian messenger arrived at the mission to issue a declaration of war.

Indians armed themselves.

Non-Indians armed themselves.

The Indians captured La Purísima. They held it for nearly a month.

Non-Indians captured seven Indian insurgents.

The insurgents could not see death coming.

Their hands were tied behind their backs and their eyes were blindfolded when they were shot.

Enraged by these executions, Indians captured Prisca, a white girl.

They could've done to her what was done to the seven. Instead, they released her.

I don't know where the seven insurgents are buried.

I do know that ʻaqi is a Chumash word. It means undertaker.

Anthropologist Alfred Kroeber studied Chumash and Costanoan languages, compiling comparative vocabulary lists.

Xuxaʼw is coyote in Samala Chumash.

Coyotl is coyote in Nahuatl.

In Nueva Galicia, caste-obsessed officials racialized some people as coyotes.

Coyotes were of Indigenous and African heritage.

Some of my ancestors were classified as coyotes.

American cartoons taught me that roadrunners always outwit coyotes.

In 1599, following the trial of a sixty-year-old Guachichil woman found guilty of turning men into coyotes, Spanish officials executed the accused witch by hanging.

Historian José Ignacio Dávila Garibi studied Coca, the Indigenous language once spoken throughout Cocollan, Chapallan, and Coinan. He compiled only a few words and phrases. One of the verbs he managed to preserve is següe, to rest.

I'm not sure how to say coyote in Coca. Dog is marri.

Dogs are honored by Cocas. They prance alongside human spirits, escorting our souls to the afterlife.

A poem that Solares shared with Harrington is titled "Dog Girl." It begins, "There were some very poor dogs:/ they scavenged to eat; refuse, they scavenged. / There were lots of children: / they grew, / they were all thin. / They were quick to make themselves stand. / They were suffering; / they scavenged bones."

In the decade before her own death, Solares dictated to Harrington what Chumash souls do upon separation from the body, making their journeys to the land of the dead across the sea: "Three days after a person has been buried, the soul comes up out of the grave in the evening. Between the third and fifth day, it wanders about the world visiting the places it used to frequent in life. On the fifth day after death, the soul returns to the grave to oversee the destruction of its property before leaving for Similaqsa. The soul goes first to Point Conception, which is a wild and stormy place.... There is a place at Humqaq below the cliff that can only be reached by rope and there is a pool of water there like a basin, into which fresh water continually drips. And there in the stone can be seen the footprints of women and children. There the spirit of the dead bathes and paints itself. Then it sees a light to the west and goes toward it through the air, and thus reaches the land of Similaqsa."

In 2007, the Tribal Elders Governing Board of the Santa Ynez Band of Chumash Indians hosted a luncheon honoring Maria Solares at the reservation's Tribal Hall. People and music filled the space, and the celebration concluded with three Indigenous language learners, Kathy Marshall, Carmen Sandoval, and Nakia Zavalla, Solares' fifth great-granddaughter, performing "Amazing Grace" in Samala Chumash, a language that lives because Maria Solares kept it that way.

Deborah Miranda, daughter of Alfred Edward Robles Miranda, a Chumash and Esselen man, writes and performs poetry. In her poem "Lies My Ancestors Told Me," she explains something that confused me when my father took us to the missions, "Give your children Spanish / names — Tranquilino, María Ignacia,/ Dolores, Faustino — / lies that deflect genocide / so tell them loudly / at the baptismal font in the Old Mission, / to the Indian Agent collecting the bodies / for the Boarding School; / broadcast the names in the street / like wheat when you call / your Mexican children in at dusk / for a bite of acorn mush / and cactus apple."

During those childhood day trips to the missions, I noticed that the Indians had names that didn't seem Indian to me. They seemed Mexican.

On the rare occasion that we did learn about Indians at school, teachers rarely named them. Only a few chiefs got that privilege. Sitting Bull. Geronimo. Crazy Horse. I was never taught the name of a single California Indian, not even the famous Ishi, the Yahi who newspapers advertised as "the last Wild Indian in California."

At school, I learned the names of many Indian-killers and Indian-killer financiers.

There are beautiful plants, like the *Fremontodendron*, named after these men. There are schools, like Stanford University, named after these men.

In *Bad Indians*, Deborah Miranda recalls a visit to Mission Dolores in San Francisco, the same city where Ishi spent his final years.

On October 14, 1911, the *San Francisco Chronicle* invited its readers to visit the Museum of Anthropology. There they could meet the "uncontaminated aborigine" recently discovered near Oroville.

"Curator A.L. Kroeber...has arranged to have Ishi on exhibition from 1 o'clock until 4. Between those hours Ishi will allow the people of the city to inspect him, weaving a fish net, chipping arrowpoints or engaged in some other native occupation."

During her visit to Mission Dolores, Miranda encountered a mother and daughter. The schoolgirl was a fourth grader, and her mom was filming her as she read from a pamphlet on mission history for a class project. When Miranda introduced herself as an Indian, the little girl got spooked.

"She stared at me as if I had risen, an Indigenous skeleton clad in decrepit rags, from beneath the clay bricks of the courtyard," writes the poet.

Let's leave California for a moment.

Let's go south.

Let's examine some nineteenth-century "Mexican" names.

On August 23, 1835, at the Church of Saint Francis of Assissi in the pueblo of Zacoalco de Torres, presbyter Don José Maria Elias baptizes my third great-grandfather, José Bernardo Escobar Sastre.

En el nombre del padre y del hijo y del Espiritu santo.

Amen.

Indigenous hands etched an animal trinity—deer, rabbits, and egrets—into the Franciscan building's facade.

In the Coca language, the tongue spoken throughout the lands of the Coca people before Spanish settlers silenced it, deer is neari. Rabbit is tuxti. Egret is...

Someone locked the Coca word for bird in a cage.

Can you help me find the key?

After my kindergarten teacher taught me the story of the first Thanksgiving, how the Indians welcomed the Pilgrims and fed them turkey and all of us should be thankful for that peaceful encounter upon which the United States of America was founded, I had questions.

When I got home, I went to the person who I believed had all the answers.

"Are we Pilgrims?" I asked my father.
    He laughed. "No."
    "Are we Indians?"
    Dad paused, getting lost in silence.
    When he finally spoke, he gave me a jumble of words about 1492 and a group of people called Chichimecas and epidemics and mass death, but all of these terrible things had happened long ago, very long ago, too long ago to matter, too long ago to discern, too long ago to recover. It was my father's long-winded way of saying that maybe, in a way, we were, and no, we're not anymore, and please, don't bring it up again.

On May 10, 1904, Jesús Calderon, the recorder in charge of Zacoalco's civil registry, writes that a local man, Exiquio Rivera, reported to authorities that Bernardo Escobar, a baker, has died of gastroenteritis. He will be buried in a pauper's grave.

On the evening of May 13, 1977, while my dad watches *Saturday Night Live*, my mom goes into labor. After wrapping her in blood-soaked bedsheets, he carries her to the Pinto. They drive to Marian Hospital. She gives birth to me at this small medical facility, the only Catholic one in Santa Maria.

The gap between Bernardo's death and my birth spans seventy-three years. He died where he was born, en el barrio de Santa Maria.

During winter, when I shape the dough to make my three kings cake, I think of Bernardo. I glance at his picture, which hangs from the perfect spot for a baker's portrait, my kitchen wall. I invite his spirit to bless my hands, my rosca, my new year, my everything.

In the margin of the church registry, where Zacoalco's presbyter recorded the details of my third great-grandfather's birth, he wrote, "José Bernardo, Indio del Barrio de Santa Maria."

In her book *Tecuexes and Cocas*, anthropologist Carolyn Baus de Czitrom identifies San Francisco Zacoalco as a Coca community.

During the sixteenth century, Zacoalco came under the administration of Nueva Galicia, a large province colonized by the Spanish crown. When missionary Domingo Lázaro de Arregui, visited, the region's biodiversity compelled him to write *Descripción de Nueva Galicia*. The priest-turned-historian explained that the native people of Nueva Galicia had a plant for everything.

Plants that supplied inexhaustible strength grew in Nueva Galicia.
Plants that cured illness grew in Nueva Galicia.
Plants that aided hunters grew in Nueva Galicia.
Plants that made sturdy and cozy habitations for humans grew in Nueva Galicia.

Plants capable of vanquishing one's enemies also grew in Nueva Galicia.

During the mid-seventeenth century, the Bishop of Guadalajara travelled Nueva Galicia. He took ethnographic notes, identifying communities where Coca populations clustered. Zacoalco, Techaluta, and San Cristóbal de la Laguna were among the thirty-four Coca pueblos that he listed.

Three Indigenous languages were spoken, and on occasion, written, in Zacoalco: Coca, Nahuatl, and Pinome. Nahuatl and Coca petitions addressed to the Spanish Crown attest to the efforts made by Indigenous people to defend their lands from thieves.

Missionaries used Nahuatl to catechize the Indians of Nueva Galicia. The language spread, silencing Coca and many others.

In 1668, an unidentified notary from Zacoalco addressed the Spanish Crown in Nahuatl. The notary concluded their grievance with the phrase "nican tlami totlatotzin."

Here end our words...

Anthropologist Francesco Zanotelli studied the cargo system that funds Zacoalco's feast of Saint Francis. In *Holy Money: Moral Finance in Two Contemporary Communities in Western Mexico*, he describes a paradox that surprised him.

Checklists to identify Indigenous people, places, and things are often developed by non-Indigenous people, such as Italian social scientists. Linguist Yásnaya Elena Aguilar Gil has written extensively about these checklists, referring to them as "indigenometers." Her concept is intentionally silly, suggesting a racialized system of weights and measures that governments can apply to quantify indigeneity.

In *Holy Money*, Zanotelli lists the typical characteristics used to determine indigeneity. When I rearticulate his criteria as a checklist, an indigenometer emerges:

–Does this person, or do these people, speak their native language? YES/NO
–Does this person, or do these people, wear traditional clothing or regalia? YES/NO
–Does this person, or do these people, rely on a traditional form of government? YES/NO
–Does this person, or do these people, believe in a unique cosmogony? YES/NO

Zanotelli stresses that in contemporary Zacoalco, the answer to each of these questions is no. However, these four 'no's' are met with a contradiction. In Zacoalco, the residents of certain barrios are treated as inferior. Self-appointed elites slur these supposed nothings, calling them "troublemakers," "pigs," and "sandal makers." They also call them by the very word that anthropologists dare not apply—"Indians."

In the essay, "Blood, Name, Surname: Indigenous Women and Nation States," Aguilar Gil writes that "in many Indigenous languages...there is no equivalent word for 'Indigenous.'"

When asked if she was Indigenous, Aguilar Gil's grandmother would answer, "No." Instead, she would answer that she is Mixe.

To be Mixe or Coca or Nahua or Chumash, one needs other Mixes, Cocas, Nahuas, or Chumash.

One also needs land.

In 1856, Indigenous cacique Lugardo Onofre addressed the natives of San Cristóbal and Zacoalco, urging them to take up arms against land thieves. In a proclamation addressed to the Mexican government, Onofre reaffirmed the autonomy of Jalisco's Indigenous pueblos. Before their plan could be executed, Mexican officials caught and executed Onofre. Wealthy landowners accused the native rebels of attempting a reverse conquest, which reminds me of the time I told a white lady to quit talking shit about Native Americans. In response, she called me a reverse racist.

A white historian who studied the attempted uprising in Zacoalco cast doubt over the existence of Lugardo Onofre.

This white historian found it hard to believe that an Indian would have such an elegant name.

This white historian found it hard to believe that an Indian could issue an eloquent political statement.

This white historian was simply being white.

Indians burdened with Mexican names no longer confuse me.

I didn't get it when I was nine.

I get it now.

So many of us have been forced to carry heavy names.

In 1984, the Department of Biological Sciences at the University of California at Santa Barbara published their third issue of *The Herbarium*. The text inventoried the botanical resources of La Purisima Mission State Historic Park. On page 75, in the section titled "Flora," the report's authors boast that the "Lompoc region has been of great interest to botanists for a long time." By "a long time," it appears that they mean since the arrival of white settlers; native people go unrecognized as scientists by the report. The authors credit the early interest in local botany to "the collections of Ida Mae Blochman, who discovered a number of endemics during her exploration of the flora during the late 19th century."

In the 1984 issue of *The Herbarium*, the word "native" appears over forty times.

In the 1984 issue of *The Herbarium*, native people are mentioned three times, always in the past tense.

When she haunts my imagination, Ida Mae Blochman assumes the form of a bouquet that combines five colonized wildflowers.

Each flower carries her name.

Ida...

Ida...

Ida...

Ida...

Ida...

The weight of the name makes their necks sag.

In her weekly wildflower column, Blochman often used the phrase "our indigenous plants."

Our.

Ida Mae Blochman, what makes these plants yours?

Should we hold a séance and ask her?

Ida Mae, which flowers are yours?

Blochman's leafy daisy...

Blochman's dudleya...

Blochman's ragwort...

Blochman's larkspur...

and

Blochman's liveforever...

MIDWINTER IN SANTA MARIA VALLEY

Santa Maria Times, Saturday, January 3, 1891

The valley and foothills are carpeted with beautiful green grass and wildflowers. We were about to forget to mention that beans and peas are also in bloom and flower gardens looking as bright, fresh, and lovely as in springtime. We do not want to give our friends in the east the California fever, but it is an actual fact that no one ever stops one year in the Santa Maria Valley and then desires to go away or live elsewhere.

THE HILL

When Dad got a raise, we moved to the house on the hill. My brother and I claimed its north-facing bedrooms. His walls were white. Mine were peach. When we gazed out our tall windows, a rural landscape hypnotized us. Row crops. A chain of foothills crowned by an amber aura. Crows silhouetted against a sky so pale it almost wasn't.

In the morning, fog hovered outside our windowpanes. This white veil reminded us that the sea was west. Garey, a quasi-ghost town that still carried the name of the citrus specialist who'd founded it, stood east. To our south rolled a storied landform, the Solomon Hills. These were named after Salomón Maria Simeon Pico, a Mexican gunslinger with a talent for vanishing into thorny chaparral.

Salomón was the cousin of Pío de Jesús Pico, the last governor of Mexican California. One of my teachers, old Mrs. Jones, would've square danced on Salomón's grave if it wasn't all the way in Mexico. She hated communists and Salomón practiced a form of wealth redistribution that probably made him one in her cataracted eyes. To hear her describe him, Salomón was the devil, a savage half-breed, or rather third-breed, who ambushed innocent horsemen and executed them, hacking off their ears with his long knife. After galloping back to his cave, Salomón rifled through his victims' saddlebags, taking inventory of the spoils. Seated before his campfire, the fiend strung freshly amputated ears on a leather cord, crafting a lobed rosary.

What hypocrisy. Old Mrs. Jones shared Salomón's alleged taste for
macabre jewelry. She taught while wearing a gold chain. From it dangled
a crucifix, the device used to torture and kill God's only son. If you looked
closely at old Mrs. Jones' cross, you could see Jesus' bony little corpse nailed
to it. Might as well wear a dead pioneer's ear.

When we drove past Salomón's lookout point, which was visible from
the freeway, Dad would point at it with his elbow. Then, he'd regale us, and
himself, with tales about the desperado whose exploits had inspired *The
Mark of Zorro,* a pulp novel featuring a fictional swashbuckler who killed with
a sword, rather than a Colt revolver. Before Salomón stalked the hills skirt-
ing the Santa Maria Valley, he'd owned Rancho de Tuolumne, a 58,000-acre
tract of land granted to Pico by Governor Manuel Micheltorena. After gold
was discovered there, forty-niners invaded and stole his ranch. Next, his
wife died. Salomón prayed for the return of his land and the resurrection of
Juana. When his prayers went unanswered, he settled for revenge, robbing
and executing white ranchers who toted sacks of gold up the King's Highway,
on their way to bank in San Francisco.

Like a good Christian, Salomón shared his loot with sickos and sinners,
Jesus' favorite people. Perched atop the area's tallest peak, the highwayman
enjoyed a falcon's-eye view of the valley, surveilling the long dirt road lined
with mustard grass that led all the way back to the church where he was bap-
tized, Mission San Juan Bautista. It's rumored that before the bandido fled to
Mexico, he buried his treasure somewhere in Los Alamos or Orcutt. I went
to Orcutt Junior High School, and the conditions on campus were so shitty
that they bred our own Salomón Pico. She was a baby-faced seventh grader
who decided that she'd had enough of white-girl cruelty. She attacked the
queen of the mean white girls with scissors. Instead of clipping one of the
bitch's ears, our teen bandit rode into the sunset with a hank of blonde hair.

I knew Zorro from comic books, movies, and TV shows. Walt Disney's
Zorro had introduced Dad and his brother to the bandit, and my brother had
gone trick-or-treating disguised as the brigand. Setting aside the fact that he
was six, my brother probably resembled the real Zorro more than the Hollywood actors cast to play him. Like many Mexican settlers, Salomón's parents were of African, Indian, and European descent. The Californio probably

looked less like Douglas Fairbanks or Erroll Flynn, two cinematic Zorros, and more like the Mexican men banned from sitting in the white section of California's segregated movie theatres.

Dad said that Salomón had fertilized the land with his victims' bodies, that that's why things grew so well in and around the Santa Maria Valley, and now that we lived on nearly an acre, who knew what, or who, lay beneath our soil.

Bullet-riddled skeletons? Gold? Oil? Gophers? Turnips?

We'd find out once we started digging.

Our white stucco house was plopped on a grassy terrace that most solicitors never saw. They were put off by our absurdly steep driveway. The only strangers brave enough to attempt the trek were the Jehovah's Witnesses who never returned after Dad "greeted" them on our porch. Beyond our back patio was another slope held in place by a short retaining wall. Altogether, our almost-acre was angled like a person doing a wall squat.

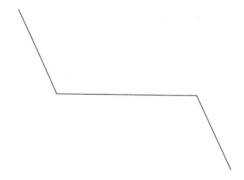

Our new house's spaciousness was great, but what thrilled Dad was the yard. Never had he thought he'd have so much land to take care of, and he had a vision for it that excluded the ice plant and pampas grass colonizing most of it. The former were a chaotic sea of rubbery, green witch fingers. The latter were big, fluffy goblins that I imagined whirling like dervishes in the moonlight while I slept. Thinking of them as enemies made it easier to dislike these plants. Dad was angry at them for what they were doing, or rather weren't doing, to the land, and I swear I saw them tremble in his presence. He planned to evict them and drop them off at the dump. They were the wrong plants for the hill.

The hill...

That's how we came to think of our home. And we knew that our home was alive. She showed us.

The hill drooled and vomited mud, clay, and silt into our street, depositing mounds of sediment that forced speeders to slow down. We were returning home with groceries, heading toward our driveway when Dad said, "Look. An alluvial fan."

"Where?"

Dad pointed. "See how the hill is spilling off the curb and into the road? That's soil erosion. The vegetation planted by the asshole who used to live here is accelerating it. Pampas grass. What a stupid choice. Just stupid. Why pampas grass? Maybe the asshole had gaucho fantasies?"

"What's a gaucho?" I asked.

"A South American vaquero."

Kicking out the ice plant and pampas grass would be our first step in securing the hill. Next, we'd replace them with vegetation that would keep our hill tight, stable, and whole. We wanted our house to remain where it was, and if the hill kept crumbling, we might wake up to find ourselves in the living room of our across-the-street neighbor. She was a blonde widow who kept a loud parrot by her bay window. Grapes destined to become pinot noir ripened in the vineyard just beyond her backyard.

TV and California had taught me about the violence of soil erosion. On the news, I'd seen rich people's homes slide down cliffs, only to be gulped by the sea. During a drive to Santa Barbara, by Gaviota Pass, I watched a mudslide eat a Toyota. Instead of feeling bad for its driver, I was awed by how the earth had satisfied her hunger. Her appetite was dynamic.

My dad's friend, a gardener who drove a dented pickup truck, helped us move into the hill. Instead of hiring his friend to assist with landscaping, Dad decided to save money. He appointed my brother, sister, and me as his work crew.

As he was leaving the bathroom one morning, I confronted Dad about our labor conditions.

"How are you going to compensate us for our work on the hill?"

"Room and board."

He was cheating us out of a wage, but I decided not to strike. What was the point? I'd lose.

For about six months, prepping the hill to receive native plants consumed my Saturdays and Sundays. My mother woke my siblings and me at dawn, and after we scarfed down our tortilla, hot dog, and bean breakfast, we prepared for battle. I returned to my peachy room and put on my oldest pants. Then, I buttoned up a flannel and slid on some busted tennis shoes. In the garage, I put on a wide-brimmed straw hat and grabbed a pair of oversized gloves. Our gloves were always too big. When our toil raised dust, we tied paisley bandanas around the lower halves of our faces. With machetes in hand, my brother, sister, and I looked ready to be initiated into Salomón's posse.

While other neighborhood kids slept until noon or watched cartoons, we wielded pickaxes, shovels, and shears. Sweat dripped down our temples, moistening our grimy necks. We wiped our brows with our sleeves and bandanas, sucked salt off our upper lips. "Hydrate! Hydrate! Hydrate!" Dad yelled at us, and we made sure to guzzle glass after glass of tap water even though it made us pee a lot. Bathroom breaks got on Dad's nerves. You can't landscape while you're on the toilet.

I hacked at ice plant and hacked at ice plant and hacked at pampas grass. No other kids in our neighborhood were at war with plants. In fact, no other kids in our neighborhood did yard work. Only grown-ups did and often, those adults were paid gardeners with trucks, gasoline-powered equipment, and lots and lots of heavy tools that I kind of wanted to fondle.

When Dad wasn't looking, I pulled off my gloves, shoved them in my back pocket, and worked bare-handed. The gloves were thick and bulky, and I got a better grip on tools and plants when I could feel them directly against my skin. Clay accumulated under my fingernails, and I imagined seeding them, using them as flower beds. I'd heard my mother accuse my brother of having ears so dirty that potatoes could grow in them. Why not roses?

WORK PROGRESSING NICELY ON NEW HIGH-POWER LINE

Santa Maria Times, Saturday, March 22, 1913

The electric current that will hereafter supply Santa Maria with light and power comes from the Sierra mountains, a distance of over 300 miles, where it is generated by the Kern River high in the mountains....

Punctuation can be earth.
^^^^^^^^^^^^^^^^^^

Punctuation can be water.
....

Punctuation can be fire.
iiiiiiiiiiiiiiiiiiiiii

Punctuation can be wind.
~~~~~~~~~~~~~~~~

IMPATIENS

At the house on Garnet Way, we planted a plum tree and a small vegetable garden. We were able to do this only after Dad cleared the gravel and pebbles from the backyard, replacing them with sod. This green cushioned my brother, sister, and me as we failed to land cartwheels, impersonated bandits, and somersaulted in front of sprinklers in July.

When vegetable gardens get attacked, possums, squirrels, and raccoons are the usual suspects. In the Garnet backyard, I became the varmint. Unable to wait for anything to sprout, I stood near the plum tree, staring at the rows we'd planted. I inched closer and closer until my hands were in the soil, fingers digging, pulling seeds back aboveground, inspecting them for signs of life. I didn't mean to, but in my impatience, I aborted an entire generation of radishes.

I don't want my anticipation to put so much pressure on my poppy seeds in the enchilada sauce can that they ghost me. My poppy-to-be needs privacy.

I can give that to her.

Louis Charles Adélaïde de Chamisso de Boncourt, the French nobleman who assigned my poppy her Linnean name, visited what would become

California's gayest city just once. That brief stay gave him enough time to linguistically scar the state's flora.

Born in 1781, the future poet and naturalist proved tender-hearted; nothing gave the sensitive child more pleasure than meeting a new plant or making an insect friend. When revolutionaries threatened to mulch France with aristocratic remains, little Louis and his parents hugged their chateau goodbye and sprinted to Germany. At fifteen, the romantic refugee Teutonised his name, becoming Adalbert von Chamisso. He enlisted in the Prussian military, went to war against his homeland, and was taken prisoner. After his release, he made his way to Berlin, where he toyed with skin and bone, studying anatomy and physiology under various instructors.

In 1814, Chamisso published *The Wonderful History of Peter Schlemihl*, a novella whose plot reminds me of Hans Christian Andersen's "The Shadow." It also reminds me of a myth Dad told me about Robert Johnson, the bluesman who struck a moonlit deal with a mischief maker he met at a Mississippi crossroads. The novella's protagonist, Peter Schlemihl, is very much Chamisso's shadow. Schlemihl travels our planet, observing. A phytophile, he boasts about studying "the kingdom of plants more profoundly than anyone else..." Chamisso did the same. After circumnavigating the globe for three years, the naturalist brought 12,000 plant species back to Russia.

The *Rurik*, a brig belonging to the Imperial Russian Navy, delivered Chamisso to California shores. The ship had set sail from Saint Petersburg in 1815, and its research expedition was financed by Count Nikolai Petrovich Rumianstev, an imperial Russian chancellor. Chamisso joined the voyage in Copenhagen and, at age thirty-four, he became the ship's most senior and stylish passenger. As the expedition's principal naturalist, Chamisso did a lot of walking, peering, staring, naming, harvesting, bothering, collecting, poking, clipping, cutting, writing, drawing, and thieving. Like Ida Mae Blochman, Chamisso was a self-taught botanist. Everyone was back then. Western botany was just a baby. A fetus. An embryo. A cotyledon.

In 1816, during the month that we welcome the return of our dead, the *Rurik* sailed into San Francisco Bay, anchoring at the harbor. Padres emerged to greet the travelers, inviting them to celebrate the feast of Saint Francis at Mission Dolores. The crew accepted. In his log, Captain Otto von Kotzebue gives a backhanded compliment to his hosts, "...it was not until we arrived in the neighborhood of the Mission that we met with a pleasant country and recognized the luxuriant scenery in California." Chamisso's botanical notes supply more detail, both praising and insulting my home state: "The prickly-leaved oak, *Quercus agrifolia*, is the most common and largest tree. With crooked boughs and entangled branches, it lies, like the other bushes, bent towards the land; and the flattened tops, swept by the sea-wind, seem to have been clipped by the gardener's shears. The flora of this country is poor... It however offers much novelty to the botanist."

Couldn't Chamisso find novelty at home?

I've never been to Berlin, but I hear that its wild.

Isn't that where Magnus Hirschfeld had his sexology museum?

During golden poppy season, these flowers blanket California. The *Rurik* docked here in the off-season, when only a few yellowish poppies punctuate our landscape. A floral ellipsis here. A floral ellipsis there. To see golden poppies blaze fiery orange in every direction, you have to be present at the height of their power: springtime. The Spanish called these annuals copa de oro, cup of gold, and in the company of Doctor Johann Friedrich von Eschscholz, the ship's physician and botanist, Chamisso botanized, harvesting samples to bring back to Russia. The *Rurik* cut across oceans with California poppy seeds jostling on board, and instead of attaching his own name to the flower, Chamisso named her after his German botanizing partner. In 1829, he published his first description of *Eschscholtzia californica*. In 1826, the poppy's profile found a bigger audience when *Linnaea* republished a lightly edited version of the piece Chamisso had written for *Horae physicae Berolineses*.

In return for honoring his surname with a golden flower, the doctor named several native and non-native plants after the naturalist. The California blackberries that ripened in the backyard of the first house I called home are *Rubus vitifolius* Chamisso. The California wildrose that I planted on the hill with my father is *Rosa californica chamissoniana*.

Tomorrow, I might eat some of these berries for lunch.

Tomorrow, I might sniff one of these roses if I find one blossoming along the Kern River.

There are historians who treat Chamisso as a compassionate colonist, a naturalist who sympathized with the plight of California Indians. It's true that he criticized the padres' treatment of the neophytes, arguing that "the contempt which the missionaries have for the people to whom they are sent seems to us, considering their pious occupation, a very unfortunate circumstance." Chamisso also commented that none of the padres bothered to learn the Indians' history, customs, religions, or language. The problem with this critique is that the naturalist failed to apply it to himself. The Frenchman-turned-German came to California and imposed language on his "discoveries," plants that had forged intimate relationships with the humans who'd been caring for them for eons. Instead of learning their names, Chamisso replaced them.

I've heard botanist Robin Wall Kimmerer say that "renaming is a powerful form of colonialism." It's a way for settlers to erase original meanings, imposing their own.

In Chumash, rose isn't a German physician. Instead, the flower is watiqoniqon.

In Chumash, blackberry isn't a German physician. The fruit is tɨqɨtɨq.

It's impossible to know who Eschscholz or Chamisso enjoyed having sex with. Still, what makes them palatable as historical figures is to imagine them as a pair of colonial fags naming flowers after each other. They become more interesting as Brokeback botanists committed to stroking delicate petals that move in silky, concentric whorls. At the heart of these petals rests a dark brown anther and at its very center, the gynoecium, *Eschscholzia californica*'s globular ovary.

Like two nervous teenagers at the movies who reach into a bucket of popcorn and graze fingers, I picture botanist and naturalist reaching for the same stem, fingertips brushing.

Each California poppy has multiple male stamens and female carpels.

Each California poppy also wears lace.

Just look at her leaves.

It's time for me to go north. Instead of poppy fields, I'm headed for forests. A spare key hides beneath a flowerpot by my front door. It's for the plant sitter who should be at my apartment right now, watering the forests and jungles growing in every room.

I trust that they'll be safe with her. I'll only be gone for a day or two.

I'm on my way to the river.

I'm on my way to be reborn.

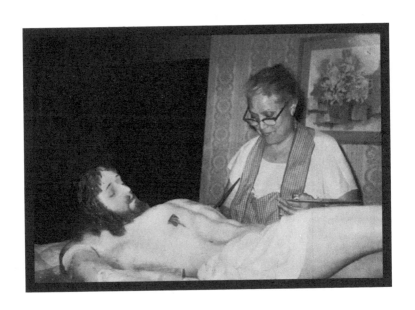

UNTITLED

Santa Maria Times, Saturday, March 9, 1895

The death of an old German in Monterey County from the effects of mushroom poisoning reminds us that there is said to be but one sure method of distinguishing mushrooms and toad stools. That test is to eat them—if they kill you, they are toad stools; if they do not, they are mushrooms....

LILIES

When I complained to Dad that we were the only kids in the neighborhood who gardened on the weekends, he raised his right hand and rubbed his thumb back and forth against his index finger.

"What are you doing?"

"This is the world's smallest violin. Can't you hear it? It's playing 'My Heart Bleeds for You.'"

One Saturday, during a lunch break from landscaping, I asked, "Dad, why do we have to do work that the other kids in the neighborhood don't have to?"

I watched my father deliberate between a dill pickle spear and a cheese square sweating on a plate in the middle of our kitchen table. Without looking away from either of these deli items, he answered, "I put my children to work so that you won't grow up to be assholes."

He bit into his briny choice and followed his wise reply with consonant clusters.

Crunch.

Crunch.

My father despised assholes. I was thankful that he was trying to prevent me from becoming one, but I questioned his methods. Wasn't there an easier way?

In Dad's world, assholes were drivers who didn't use their turn signals. Cyclists who cut off cars. Dog owners whose dogs were always off leash and frosting yards with baroque turds. Cats. Our mayor, governor, and president composed a trinity of elected assholes. The most controversial figure to be ascribed this nomenclature was Dad's nemesis and father-in-law, Ricardo Serrano Ríos.

During his peasant childhood, my grandfather collected firewood from the pine and oak forests surrounding the canyon he called home. Morning glory bursting with purple flowers wrapped itself around trunks, twigs, branches, and stumps. Glossy nightshade dangled large ebon berries. Armies of mushrooms brought a soft, meaty texture to felled logs, exposed roots, and otherwise crunchy forest floors.

Crunch.

Crunch.

My grandfather was born and raised in Villa Guerrero, a rural municipality where kids grow up foraging, eating, and playing with mushrooms, throwing the big puffy ones at each other the way kids in frozen places fight with snowballs.

Mexico is one of this planet's most mushroom-rich countries. It hosts diverse psilocybin fungi. Many of these grow best in ethereal settings—cloud forests.

The shape and color of *Amanita muscaria* inspired the red-capped toadstool emoji. This fungus fruits in Villa Guerrero. The southern Tepehuanes call it tirok yakua, a nod to the slight reptilian texture marking the species's cap. The Wixaritari give a foreboding name to this creature, yekwá 'itaikarieya. That second word roughly translates to "ghost," which is what might visit you if you accidentally binge on these fun guys. Only shamans have the spiritual expertise to handle the visions and visitations provoked by a mouthful of fly agaric.

Fungal foragers impress me. One small mistake could cost them their souls.

Fly agaric's killer cousin, *Amanita phalloides*, hitched a ride on an unknown tree, possibly an oak, and arrived in California just before the gold rush. Writer Shirley Jackson uses this fungus as a foreshadowing device in her venomous novel, *We Have Always Lived in the Castle*: "My name is Mary Katherine Blackwood. I am eighteen years old.... I like my sister Constance, and Richard Plantagenet, and *Amanita phalloides*, the death-cap mushroom. Everyone else in my family is dead."

My grandfather's bones rest in el Panteon de Mezquitan.
　　So do his parents'.

My great-grandmother Magdalena turns to dust alongside her own marijuana prince.

They met at a river.

Magdalena stands belly-button-deep in the water, bathing herself.
In her peripheral vision, movement.
She turns to look.
A man. He's staring.
"You!" he announces. "You are going to be my wife."
Magdalena abandons her clothes on the riverbank, sprints home, and hides.
She sits on the ground and rocks back and forth. She's trembling.
She tells no one about the stranger who saw her naked.
She tells no one about the stranger's announcement.
When Magdalena's mother sends her back to the river with laundry, the stranger reappears, this time mounted on a horse. When Magdalena sees him, she again abandons the clothes and runs. The stranger spurs his horse, forcing the animal to chase his prey. Once he's close enough to touch the child, the raptor grabs her by her waist and places her astride his horse.
Gumecindo takes his captive to his sister's house.
There he makes the necessary arrangements for Magdalena to become his under the law.

According to one of my great-uncles, Gumecindo was eighteen years his bride's senior. On their marriage certificate, a civil servant recorded his age. Twenty-eight. He wrote hers too.

Nineteen.

I never met Magdalena, and yet I think of her often.
I've heard that she was shorter than my mother.

I've heard that she wore her hair in a long black braid that tickled her waist.

A cloud forest crowned her.

Smoking tobacco soothed her. So did telling stories.

I learned about the god Xochipilli, the Mexica Prince of Flowers, from a book about the Aztecs that my mom gave me for my eighth birthday. I marveled at the photograph of the god's statue. It had been unearthed from a volcano, Mount Popocatépetl. Xochipilli is part man and part plant, and the sculptor who adorned his body with tobacco, morning glory, and mushrooms shaped these entheogens with care. I wondered about the look on his face. Equal parts pain, equal parts ecstasy.

José Maria Nuñes might sound like a Mexican name, but his birth predates Mexico. José Maria was Magdalena's great-grandfather. He was the son of Marcos Nuñes and Feliciana Lopes, two "indios" who appear and reappear in the church registry of Huejúcar, a military settlement founded by Tlaxcaltecas. During the sixteenth century, these Nahua colonizers trekked up from the south and received privileges from the Spanish Crown in exchange for services. Their duties? To police and subdue the Chichimecas, a catchall term for the nations populating Nueva Galicia's northern frontier.

This was a case of natives colonizing natives on behalf of non-natives.

That was how the conquest happened, it was native-led, and I like how historian Federico Navarrete puts it.

He says that we've been trained to think about the Spanish invaders as adventurers who took the Americas by themselves. The reality is that the conquistadors were entirely dependent on Indigenous people for survival. Without Indigenous people, especially Indigenous women, they wouldn't have known where they were, where they were going, who to talk to, or how to talk to them.

The Tlaxcaltecas brought Nahuatl with them.

Huejúcar, land of the willow trees...

Land.

The Nahua settlers of Huejúcar were granted title to communally held lands.

Local Spanish settlers were constantly trying to take it.

Like the natives of Zacoalco, the natives of Huejúcar sued.

They won.

But...

...in 1754, things really started to fall apart.

A cohort of men from Huejúcar fought to hold elections locally instead of at the cabecera, Colotlán.

Tension between Indigenous caciques mounted.

In the 1770s, Spanish officials took advantage of this tension. They attacked.

Nahua governors denounced the viceroy.

He demanded everyone's corn. All he did was extort.

The Crown responded to the natives' complaints by installing an even shittier viceroy.

Fearful for their lives, residents fled Huejúcar.

That's how José Maria went from landed to landless, cornful to cornless.

Huejúcar, land of the willow trees...

"At flood's edge yonder in Tlaxcala, let him sing narcotic flower songs," goes one Nahua ballad dedicated to the pleasures of Xochipilli.

Trinie Dalton's "Fungus Mental Telepathy" is my favorite mushroom short story. It's about psilocybin poachers, and in a single paragraph, Dalton crochets connections between Nahua botany and stoner hippie jewelry and Sylvia Plath's poetry. She enlaces a mycelium network made of cultural artifacts that might be unfamiliar to you but are super familiar to me.

Chicken of the woods is my favorite California mushroom. It tastes like most menu items from El Pollo Loco, a popular charbroiled poultry franchise.

The world's largest living organism lurks just north of California. It's a fungus covering 2,200 acres in Oregon. Some people call this monster the honey mushroom. I call it the humongous fungus.

I learned from one of the botany manuals that Dad left littered around the house that California has the largest trees in the world. The bathroom seemed to draw these books close, the toilet drew them closer, magnetizing them, causing a library to mushroom on top of the porcelain tank. When I forgot to bring my Aztec book to the bathroom to help me poop, I'd reach for one of Dad's plant tomes and make caca while reading about yerba mansa, toyon, California grape, and coyote brush.

Irritable bowels played a part in teaching me about California's flora and fauna.

When I told Dad that he was developing an addiction to books about native vegetation, he reminded me that we would be filling the hill with it. When I asked him what was so special about these plants, he said, "Water, honey. They drink less water."

Water.

In California, everything, and I mean everything, always comes back to water.

I silently questioned Dad's newfound affection for water-wise landscaping. I speculated that his motive had less to do with a love of California and more to do with his feelings toward my grandfather.

My grandfather was once the loudest member of the Lerma Basin-Lake Chapala Foundation, an organization established to defend Mexico's largest freshwater lake.

The Lerma River, which empties into Chapala, is one of the world's filthiest estuaries. Kids are cautioned not to light matches near it.

My grandfather and Ramón Rubín, author of *The Lost Canoe*, both sat on the Committee for the Conversation of Lake Chapala. Like Rubín, my grandfather was also a writer, and he published a small independent newspaper called *The Report*.

My grandfather reported on himself, spreading news about the ecological good deeds he did for the people of Jalisco.

Scholars Ofelia Pérez Peña and Gabriel Torres Gonzalez wrote an essay about Ramón Rubín's literary output.

My grandfather's ghost haunts their essay's first footnote.

"...among the lake's early defenders is another impressive figure, Ricardo Serrano, who never tires of expressing his despair over Chapala's situation at every forum he attends. Because of this, he is frequently described by many politicians and National Water Commission officials as the man who 'waters down the holidays.'"

Instead of spending time with his family—or rather, families—during holidays, my grandfather was busy yelling at Jalisco's governor about water. He was Wordsworthian, wandering like a cloud, raining on everyone else's parade.

My dad says that my grandfather's commitment to the lake was motivated by guilt and ego.

By attaching himself to the lake, by becoming its most dramatic barnacle, my grandfather made himself matter.

Unlike my father, I have to hand it to my grandfather. That man understood how history, and historiography, work. My grandfather understood that sometimes, to become part of history, you have to write yourself into it.

My dad says that my grandfather should have loved my grandmother like he loved Lake Chapala. Instead, he betrayed his vows to her and controlled her and kept her poor and pregnant. He polluted her, infecting her with organisms that he brought home from strange, wet caves.

Ramón Rubín wrote about Chapala's invasive aquatic plant, the water lily. He described this flower as a useless thing which, like all useless things, deceives, tricking those who see it into believing that it's fertile, prolific, and most importantly, ambitious.

I sometimes burst into tears thinking about my grandmother Arcelia. She was as important as Chapala. Her memory remains as precious as Chapala. She liked to paint lilies. Cala lilies.

Was my grandfather my grandmother's marijuana prince?

How many of us have survived marijuana princes?

Maybe the better question is, "How many of us haven't?"

My mother's little sister once walked me to Chapala's shore. We climbed into a small boat, paid our fare, and slowly floated in the direction of Michoacán.

It was undeniable; the lake was sick. Possibly dying. There were rings around it, lines along the shore that indicated where its water levels once rose. The helmsman pointed at the glass window on the bottom of his boat and said, "There's nothing to see anymore. Our lake has been strangled by water lilies. They're killing our fish."

Next, he told us about someone who's part fish, Michi-Cihuali, the temperamental mermaid who's lived in Lake Chapala since forever. She's the boss of the lake's fish and weather, and she has a taste for human blood, the only food that will quell her tantrums. As the helmsman prattled on, I imagined this fish woman tangled in water hyacinth, naked from the waist up, thrashing. Then, I visualized my grandfather wriggling out of his serape, flinging it aside, and diving into the shallow lake. He wades to the mermaid and rescues her, dragging her to shore, where he performs mouth-to-mouth resuscitation. Once the fish woman comes to, her tail swats and throttles him.

"This is for Arcelia!" she growls, fins balled into fists, barracuda fangs ready.

Was Dad using water to one-up my grandfather?

To one-up my dad, was my grandfather going to have to save the world?

Were these men having a water fight of monumental proportions?

Was I implicated?

I pondered these questions while pretending to be a ravenous mergirl thrashing in our bathtub.

My grandfather never once visited us in California. I knew, and Dad knew, that he would never see our water-wise gardens.

We prepared to plant them anyways.

Once we finished uprooting and purging the hill's pampas grass and ice plant, we watered the soil and let it rest.

It was tired.

So were we.

Let it be

fallow.

MERMAID

I leave my dress and sandals on a rock before wading in. Once I'm waist-deep in the water, I pinch my nose and plunge into the cold until I'm submerged.

One azquil.

Two azquiles.

Three azquiles.

Four azquiles.

Five azquiles.

When I come back up for air, I wipe my eyes, rubbing the muck out of my lashes, blinking until Kern County returns to focus.

I received instructions to come here.

A priestess trained in the oracular arts dictated them to me, saying, "Write this down or remember it...."

TRIP THRU RARE SCENIC WONDERS:
Beauties of Little-Known Section of Sierra Delight Motorists

Santa Maria Times, Saturday, April 6, 1918

Miss Barbara Livingston, an Eastern friend of mine, who is touring the state at present, recently visited me with a most interesting tale of her latest excursion. This was to the Kern River country, one of the most beautiful spots in the state, but very little known to the California motorist....

YORUBA

A curandera wearing gold grills recommended that I speak with the priestess who advised me to see the river. I met this stylish healer at a party, the first one I'd attended in years. My plants gave me the courage to go. They wanted some alone time anyways. The partygoers were mostly writers and artists, and I stuck close to the vegetable tray, compulsively gnawing at carrot and celery sticks. A landscaper who I've known for years had invited me. I was her plantonic date.

Once I'd eaten half of the crudité, I grabbed a glass of rosé, chugged it, refilled it, and then wandered into the backyard, parking myself on one of the Acapulco chairs by the infinity pool. The curandera sat beside me and introduced herself as Claudia. She told me about her job as an art dealer and complained about the difficulties she was having with an upcoming show. I must've zoned out because at one point during our small talk, Claudia quieted, looked me dead in the eye, gently touched my knee, and whispered, "When was the last time you took a spiritual bath?"

Light-headed from the rosé, I hiccupped. Then, I answered, "Never. Do you bathe your spirit?"

"Yes. I can give you an herbal recipe."

"Why should I trust you?"

Claudia gave me a sympathetic smile and said, "You remind me of the way I was." Then, she leaned closer and spoke to me about how she developed her gifts as a healer, emphasizing her ability to diagnose spiritual ailments, like soul loss.

"You need help," she said.

"Is it that obvious?"

"No." She flashed a twenty-four-karat grin. "But I can see it. I have an eye for it."

Claudia tapped her forehead.

Before I left the party, she gave me the phone number of her godmother, a priestess of Shango.

"Call my madrina," she said. "Have her read for you."

Claudia hugged me.

I felt like I'd been plunged into a bath of warm rose water.

I sat at the dining room table of the priestess while she examined cowrie shells. She scooped them back up, shook them between her hands, and threw them again. They landed, scattering across a straw mat. As she interpreted the messages communicated by the shell patterns, the priestess chewed the inside of her cheek.

"You need to sweeten yourself," she said.

"How?"

"Write this down or remember it. Take flan, sunflowers, a pumpkin, and some honey to a river."

"Which river?"

"Any river. You're going to present these gifts to Oshun. Do you know who she is?" I didn't know much about Santería, but I knew the bare bones about Oshun, that she's the Yoruba deity of beauty, love, and fertility.

"She lives in the water, right?"

"She *is* the water. Fresh water. Sweet water. She purifies."

Eager to make my body a sweet home for my soul, I agreed to deliver gifts to this riverine spirit.

"Bring a change of clothes with you. You're going to get in the water—"

"I'm getting in the water?"

"Yes. You're going to take off all your clothes and you're going to get in the water. Then, you're going to talk to Oshun. Tell her everything. Everything. Don't ask for anything. Just tell her why you're there and about what happened to you. Once you're done, leave your old clothes. Put on the new ones and leave.

Do not look back."

I thanked the priestess, paid her fee, and went home.

That night, I booked a place to stay, packed, and told my plants about the instructions for my rebirth, my sweetening. I promised them that I wouldn't be gone for long and that when I returned, I'd probably be a better plant friend. That was what I hoped.

SHOT A BEAR

Santa Maria Times, Saturday, July 19, 1913

A.H. Cooley of the fire department is the high chief bear hunter of the city, says the Santa Barbara Independent. Friday of last week he left for the upper waters of the Santa Ynez on a bear hunt and Tuesday afternoon word was received from his camp that he had succeeded in bringing down a cinnamon bear....

DEN

My Airbnb is teeming with bears.

Smiling teddy bears sit cross-legged on the plaid pull-out couch facing the TV. Three crooked bear posters captioned with the words STRENGTH, RESILIENCE, and DETERMINATION are tacked to the living room's sole windowless wall. A big cardboard bear head is mounted above the fireplace. A smaller head guards the fridge. The kitchen backsplash is a tiled mosaic depicting a fairy tale family. Mama bear. Papa bear. Baby bear.

Where are they keeping Goldilocks?

In the bathroom, I thrust bear-track toilet paper into my crotch and wipe. After washing my hands, I dry them with an astoundingly bear-free washcloth.

Or is it?

It is brown.

Two glass jars gleam beside the lotion dispenser. One is filled with gummy bears. The other has a misspelled label. *Baar droppings.* Chocolate-covered raisins? Hoping that it'll be lime flavored, I try a green grizzly gummy. It tastes like an apple born in a test tube.

I spit the gelatinous animal into an empty trash can.

My Bearbnb is a condo in Visalia.

Its décor reminds me of a song that used to keep me up at night.

Dad got scolded for trying to serenade us with it when he took us to meet a celebrity tree at Sequoia National Park.

I belly flop onto a paw-print bedspread and text the priestess.

I tell her that after I put my new clothes and flip flops on, I returned to my car and drove away from the Kern River. When I pulled back onto the asphalt, a vulture descended, flapping toward me. I thought she was going to soar over my car—that's what they usually do—but this one swooped low and flew at the windshield, getting her face so close to the glass that she was able to lock eyes with me before jerking up to avoid death. A second and then a third and then a fourth and then a fifth vulture did the same, each one aiming herself at the windshield, revealing her haggard face before shooting back up at the sun.

I crack my knuckles. Yawn. Yawn again. Yawn again.

After curling into a ball, I take a deep breath. Let it out slowly. I linger in the space between wakefulness and sleep, waiting for the priestess to say something about the scavengers.

Dad had carried on the family tradition of driving his kids to the mountains so that we could hang out with famous trees, and I felt a mix of good nerves and bad nerves the summer morning that we piled into the minivan and set off for the Sierra Nevada. If a normal person had been driving, we could've made it to our campsite in about four hours. Instead, our father was in charge. While he has many gifts, a sense of direction isn't one of them. The man lacks an internal compass.

After handing Mom the atlas, Dad assigned her the role of navigator. We motored east. She repeated simple directions. Derecho. Derecho. Derecho. Tension built, once turns had to be made. Dad followed Mom's directions, but somewhere in Kings County, he glanced at her lap and roared, "YOU'RE HOLDING THE MAP UPSIDE DOWN!"

My brother, sister, and I cowered.

Mom slammed the atlas shut. The worst sound in the world followed. Have you ever wanted to kill your father for making your mother cry? We travelled in silence until a sign helped us out.

Mom read the name of the town out loud: "Lost Hills...Estamos perdidos."

I clapped my hand over my mouth so that I wouldn't laugh. It was too perfect.

Lost fucking hills.

I no longer needed to kill my father.

My mother already had.

Dad surrendered, pulling into a gas station and parking at a pump. He entered the station store empty-handed and emerged with four ice cream sandwiches and a plan to get us unlost.

When Dad was in college, he worked as a counselor at a summer camp in the San Bernardino Mountains. It was near Santa's Village, a North Pole-themed amusement park where tourists could pet reindeer and eat gingerbread all year round. One of Dad's jobs at the camp was to lead kids in campfire songs, and he made sure that his own kids learned the classics, standards like "This Land Is Your Land," "On Top of Old Smokey," "She'll be Comin' 'Round the Mountain," and the punishing "John Jacob Jingleheimer Schmidt."

During early evening car rides through the countryside, we would sing these songs as a family. I sat behind my dad, staring out the window at moonlit California live oaks, their three-hundred-year-old trunks knotted with burls, acorn-heavy boughs held high. Quercus agrifolia is a feminine life-form, a wise bitch who's both tree and witch, and I wanted to woo her, court her, bring her honey and green ribbons and silver-plated vanity mirrors so that she might admire her own beauty.

"You're gorgeous," I wanted to whisper into her lobed leaves. "May I hold your hand?"

Assholes tell women that their beauty fades after forty. Oaks prove that's bullshit. They don't come into their beauty until they're at least a hundred. Plant society is filled with sexy and sedentary centenarians who ripen and rot in defiance of human beauty standards.

During our car rides through the countryside, Dad occasionally sang "Julianne," an eerie folk song that told the story of a girl and her two-timing lover. He's a miner who promises that he's going to the mountain to fetch silver that he'll use to fashion rings. Instead, he does like my grandfather and spends the night with another girl. The next day, when the lover returns to Julianne's cabin, she's gone.

Someone has torn her door off its hinges.

Her badly mauled dog moans in pain.

Pieces of broken rifle are strewn across the floor.

The song warns that you may see Julianne in the moonlight, that she wears silver rings on her fingers and a crown of sorrow on her head, and I'd wonder about what that looked like, whether sorrow was silver, copper, or gold. Back home, after we'd brushed our teeth and put on our pajamas, I'd lie in bed, staring at the popcorn ceiling, wondering about the fate of the bear that had eaten Julianne. Had she fed herself to him on purpose?

Once we got to our campsite, we unloaded our stuff and carried it to our lodgings. These took the form of a single room with canvas walls, a canvas ceiling, and a dirt floor. A tent but sturdier. We set our sleeping bags on cots, took turns using the camp toilet, and then went for a walk.

I'd anticipated seeing a lot of plants and animals in Sequoia.

I hadn't anticipated seeing so much traffic.

At bedtime, we sang a few songs. For the grand finale, Dad started to sing "Julianne."

My sister burst into tears.

Our mom said, "Roberto, no."

He quieted but it was too late.

None of us slept.

Our imaginations teemed with bears.

Lack of sleep can derange people, and I may have gone a little crazy after that first insomniac night in Sequoia. The next day, I fell in love with every plant and animal and rock and speck of dirt in the park. I also felt deliciously small. Microscopic. That's to be expected when you meet the tallest trees in the world, trees that no human can make eye contact with. We stood at the feet of the General Sherman, staring up at his unseeable and unknowable head. If I could have, I would've asked for his autograph. The park vibrated with life. I vibrated with it. I channeled Saint Francis, talking to flowers, birds, deer, and dewdrops.

One of the tour guides who led us on a nature walk got on my nerves. He was knowledgeable but he acted like the park was a museum and he kept telling us not to touch anything. He also kept repeating that we couldn't take anything with us. Not a rock, not a twig, not a pine needle, not an anything or an anyone. He kept saying, "If everyone who visits the park takes one rock, then there'll be no more rocks." When he told us not to steal anything for the twelve-thousandth time, I snapped.

Treat people like thieves and they become thieves.

I bent down, snatched the first pine cone I saw, and shoved it in my pocket.

Rubbing its bristles relaxed me, comforting me so effectively that I forgot I'd stolen it.

When we got home, I was reminded of the cone as I helped Mom with the laundry.

"What's this?" she asked, showing me my stolen seeds.

I decided not to lie. "I took it from Sequoia."

"Go put it by the petrified wood," she said.

A chime.

I check my phone.

It's a text from the priestess.

She says that the vultures are good, very good.

I ask why.

She answers that Oshun has avatars. When she delivers petitions to the creator, she takes the form of a vulture.

I tremble at this news.

I want to cry.

But I'll wait.

I'm going to go weep among the sequoias.
    I'm going to repay them with grateful tears.

BERKELEY WOMAN WINS PASSAGE OF POPPY BILL

Berkeley Gazette, Tuesday, March 3, 1903

The golden poppy is now the official State flower, Governor Pardee having signed the bill designating it as California's floral emblem. Senator Smith of Los Angeles and Assemblyman Bliss of Alameda, who introduced the measure, placed a heap of poppies on the desk of the presiding officer of the Senate last night.... Mrs. J.G. Lemmon of Berkeley, representing the organization that asked for the enactment, was escorted to a seat beside the presiding officer, and at Senator Smith's request, Senator Shortridge presented her with the gold-mounted quill with which Governor Pardee put his name on the bill....

LEMMONS

Sometimes, you just know things.

I know that when I get home, I'll see my poppy in full bloom.

I can't explain how I know this.

I just do.

I used to stare at a poppy drawing during breakfast.

She was one flower among many.

In Sequoia, Dad had bought us a souvenir, a California native wildflowers poster. When we got home, he took it to the mall and had it framed. He hung it in the dining room, by some clay plates hand-painted with happy rabbits, deer, and nopales.

During mealtimes, when conversation turned boring, I studied the wildflowers.

The poppy was in the middle.

I'm glad that my father brought wildflowers to our every meal.

I'm glad that my father, a super-imperfect man, brought wildflowers to our every meal.

Sara Allen Plummer Lemmon lobbied the State of California to adopt the golden poppy as our official flower.

Sara got her citrus-y surname from John Gill Lemmon, a fellow botanist who she met in a city that shares its name with a soap opera, *Santa Barbara*.

Following their nuptials, the Lemmons went on a honeymoon that Sara described as a "grand botanical raid into Arizona."

Sara was like Ida Mae Blochman, another white schoolmarm from Maine who settled in the West, fell in love with its native plants, became a citizen scientist, and then took things.

When John courted Sara, he wooed her by naming a shrubby plant after her.

The Spanish called this plant yerba del aire.

Ethnologist J.P. Harrington recorded Chumash uses for this plant.

Wili'lik.

Today, the species is recognized as *Baccharis plummerae*.

I call this plant coyote brush.

Coyote brush cloaks the hills where Salomón Pico relieved cattlemen of their gold.

Coyote brush scraggled along the barbed wire fences enclosing the cattle who stared at our minivan as we rumbled past their pastures.

I once saw coyote brush holding hands with toloache.

Our father taught us to never fuck with toloache.

We were in the countryside on a rock harvesting expedition. Dad had pulled over and my sister and I were helping him load stones into the van.

Near a roadside shrine, I saw a plant with resplendent green leaves and long-necked white flowers, angelic trumpets.

With a pointy finger, the plant beckoned for me to come close.

I went to shake his spooky hand.

"Get back here!" Dad yelled.

I jumped. He'd never screamed at me for being friendly to a plant.

"Why?"

"That's jimson weed. It's dangerous."

"Why?"

"If you play with that plant, you'll meet God.

Are you ready to meet God?"

Unprepared to meet our maker, I backed away from the tempting white flowers.

Toloache flashed me a sly smile.

I respect Toloache by keeping my distance from him.

He's a magician capable of revealing secrets that aren't for me.

When Sara Lemmon wrote about plants, she likened them to insects and animals, never magicians.

She made plants out to be things.

Its.

"It has fine green leaves like the locust, only not half as large, and at the touch, the pairs of leaves close. The flower is round, and pink, fine like the head of a mouse ear..."

When Lemmon wrote about native people, she chose adjectives that stabbed.

These are adjectives that she used to describe the Indians she encountered during her "botanical raid into Arizona."

Sly.
Dirtiest.
Treacherous.
Cruel.
Degraded.

I'm glad that Sara's married name was Lemmon.

She and her husband sour botanical history.

The Lemmons were friendly with another botanical couple, Mr. and Mrs. John Muir.

Mr. Muir acted the same way about national parks that that annoying tour guide did.

He wanted the parks turned into photosynthetic museums.

I haven't been back to Muir Grove until today.

When I finish giving the grove's sequoias my tears, I'm returning to the hill.

I have a gift for the hill monster.

ELEMENTARY BOARD NAMES NEW BILINGUAL DIRECTOR

Santa Maria Times, Friday, July 18, 1980

Bob Gurba, 33, a Title I resource teacher at El Camino Junior High School for the past two years, was named as the new Director of Bilingual Education for the Santa Maria Elementary School District by the Board of Education Thursday night.

Gurba, a five-year veteran of the district, was appointed to the $25,543 a year job with high praise. Board member Tom Urbanski said he thought Gurba was "far and away the best candidate for the post."

"He certainly has all the skill and the technical ability in bilingual education, and I don't think there's any questions about his ability both in the academic and administrative areas," said district Personnel Director Paul Major.

Gurba was picked from three finalists, the other two coming from outside the district. He has a master's degree in ESL. He spent five years teaching bilingual education in Mexico and speaks Spanish, English and Russian.

Gurba is married and has a three-year-old daughter.

The other major item on Thursday's agenda was a report by a group of El Camino Junior High School parents about what they feel is the school's reputation of having lower expectations of its students and being a "bad boy" campus....

STICK FIGURE

The worst moments of my life have been midwifed by men.

The marijuana prince represents the entirety of them.

There is no singular marijuana prince.

Obviously.

The only place you'll find him as a unified character is here, in this labyrinth.

He's an allegorical plant-man.

He induces mild psychedelia and near-death experiences.

The idea for him came to me in a dream...

I'm visiting a house I've never been to before.

I sit on a sofa.

A potted hemp plant squats on the end table.

I use the word squats because the plant seems to have legs. Really muscular legs.

I'm having a conversation with someone.

Movement in my peripheral vision.

The plant is standing.

He's a hemp man!

He steps off the end table, onto the wood floor, and strides away...

Do you remember the Jolly Green Giant, that vegetable company mascot?

The marijuana prince looked like him but weedier.

The purpose of this labyrinth is the prince's exile.

I want him to remain here forever.

I want for this garden, this maze, this infinite field of corn, to be his grave.

Don't let him escape.

Have you despaired over your soul's salvation?
Have you failed to receive spiritual guidance?
Have you failed to do penance for your sins?
Have you put off your penitence for too long?
Have you violated your promise to stop sinning?
Do you plan on continuing to worship the crow?
Will you continue to spread superstitions about the bird-god?

—Eighteenth-century confessional script
for Nueva Galicia's Nahuatl speakers

COYOTE BRUSH

Some of the best moments of my life were midwifed by a man.

My dad.

He taught me to read.

When determining how he'd landscape the hill, he visited plant nurseries and botanical gardens for advice and inspiration.

I was his wingman.

I rode in the passenger seat, soaking up every word he had to share about plants.

I received lectures on lemonade berry, coffeeberry, coyote brush, Christmas berry, ceanothus, monkeyflower, flannel bush, Catalina cherry, Monterey pine, Matilija poppy, a bunch of different manzanitas...

Oaks.

The more that I learned about California native plants, the deeper I fell in love with them.

I fell in love with California again and again.

I fall more in love with California every day.

I cleaned the minivan between plant runs. I operated the hand vac, sucking up all the dirt and leaves left by our new friends. I didn't mind cleaning up after them.

Please let me be vulnerable. I want to share a failure with you. My failure as a writer.

I can't describe for you the ecstasy I felt planting the hill.

But you might be able to feel what I felt if you do this:

Think of the time that plants made you happiest.

Or most yourself.

Figure out how to access that feeling. Let it move through you. Nurture it. Maintain it.

Allow that feeling to remain for as long as you can.

My father and I spent weeks digging holes, filling them with water, prepping soil, prepping root systems, easing native plants into the earth, refilling holes, saturating soil with water, letting roots know that we cared about them and wanted to feed them. Letting roots know that we loved them.

I confess: When we finished, I felt slight disappointment.

The oaks that I had the hots for were decades old.

The oaks that we'd planted were my age.

Babies.

I'd be dead by the time they'd be old enough for me to have crushes on.

I wondered if there was something I could do to make them grow faster.

There wasn't.

My affection shifted from the very young oaks to our flannel bush.

This beauty looked as if a hibiscus and some ivy had had a baby. Her tentacles were camouflaged with dark green leaves. Her neon yellow flowers reminded me of star fruit. Her pollen made me itch. She was so messy.

We had to walk with care on the hill.

Dad installed a drip irrigation system for watering our plants.

When my brother, sister, and I played kickball in our front yard, the ball sometimes rolled off the grass and down the hill.

My brother had given his soccer ball a good kick.

It disappeared.

He was reluctant to go get it.

"Want me to get it?" I asked.

"Yes, please."

My brother was scared of the hill.

Dad told us that a dangerous creature lived there.

The hill monster roamed at night, looking for naughty children.

Dad never specified what the hill monster did to these bad kids.

My brother's imagination conjured terrible punishments.

I told him, "I'll get the ball."

While I was on my way to the shrub where our ball had gotten stuck, I paid my respects to the hill monster.

"I'll be gone soon," I whispered.

I froze.

Hmmmmmmmm....

I took a few more steps toward our ball.

The humming got louder.

Bees swarmed the coyote brush.

A hive hung from one of her fluffy branches.

Papyrus stuffed with honey.

My mouth watered.

I ran.

MIXTECO ACTIVISM TURNS TO STRIKES

Santa Maria Times, Saturday, May 29, 1999

Santa Maria Valley strawberry-pickers launched wildcat strikes and began a work stoppage Friday, including laborers on a tenant farm belonging to the family of Assemblyman Abel Maldonado.

The United Mixteco Farmworkers of Santa Maria threatened to strike if their demands for higher wages are not met, and an organizer for the United Farm Workers of Santa Maria threatened to strike if their demands for higher wages are not met. An organizer for the United Farm Workers union arrived from Oxnard Friday night to discuss what further labor actions the workers might take.

Organization leader Pedro Lopez said the pickers want $2 per flat, about 60 cents more than they are currently paid.

About 1,500 Mixtecan Indians from the Mexican state of Oaxaca work strawberry farms in the valley....

THAT MEXICAN

If you open a standard Spanish-to-English dictionary and look up the word "fresa," it will likely offer strawberry as the fruit's English equivalent.

If you open a Mexican Spanish-to-English dictionary and look up the word "fresa," it will give you a different equivalent.

"Stuck up bitch."

"Rich girl."

"Middle-class brat."

If you ask me to define "fresa," I'll answer that strawberries were the ushers who led us to the hill.

My father and mother taught the children of farmworkers who harvested strawberries and other crops in the Santa Maria Valley.

Like Ida Mae Blochman, my father left the classroom to become an administrator.

First, he was chosen to be the director of bilingual education for the school district.

Then, he was chosen to be the director of the Migrant Education Program.

The program's slogan alluded to our valley's crop yields.

"A harvest of hope..."

We moved to the house on the hill after Dad began directing the Migrant Education Program.

The job came with a raise.

When I explained my dad's new job to my girls-only club members, I told them what he had told my brother, sister, and me.

Dad said that it was the responsibility of every single teacher in this country to give kids a good education. He said that some teachers were assholes, that they didn't want to give a good education to all kids. He said that these bigots discriminated against the children of migrant farm workers and that it was basically his job to force these racists to do their jobs.

My father had his enemies. Teachers who didn't refer to him by name.

They called him "that Mexican."

I thought of my dad as a local celebrity.

Everywhere we went former students chirped, "Hello, Mr. Gurba!"

Sometimes he had to ask their name. Once he got that, he always remembered them.

Some of Dad's students became strawberry sharecroppers.

One of these students would climb our steep driveway lugging crates of strawberries.

Dad sheepishly accepted these gifts.

My brother and I baked pies.

During the 1980s, most of Santa Barbara County's strawberry production took place in Santa Maria.

In 1987, Santa Maria's strawberry production was valued at $60.8 million.

A report prepared by the California Institute for Rural Studies in 1988 found that a significant number of farmworkers in and around Santa Maria lived in "substandard housing."

I didn't need to read a report to know these things. I lived in Santa Maria. I saw it.

When it fully dawned on me that strawberries *and* racism had brought us to the house on the hill, I felt weird.

As I got older, I felt even weirder about it.

As my father climbed the administrative ranks, I became fresa, a very privileged girl.

My dad's workaholism partially led to his success.

Though he worked hard, farmworkers work harder.

Harvesting strawberries is a labor-intensive task.

It breaks backs.

It seemed unfair to me that I should live in a big house paid for by my father's advocacy.

Why was he receiving this money?

Couldn't that money go directly to farmworkers?

To better understand what was happening with strawberries and wages and sharecropping and funding and school segregation in Santa Maria, I paid close attention when Dad held meetings with farmworkers and labor organizers and rural legal-defense attorneys.

Books helped me too.

In our garage, I found a copy of *The Communist Manifesto*.

I read it.

In our garage, I found a copy of *The Pedagogy of the Oppressed*.

I read it.

In our garage, I found a copy of *Savage Inequalities*.

I read it.

These three books brought into focus what my dad was doing.

I still felt weird about our big house though.

Was I supposed to thank the strawberries for bringing me to the hill?

Naomi, the member of our girls-only club who introduced me to her dad's pornography collection, was descended from Japanese strawberry-farmers.

Amber, the member of our girls-only club who sang "In the Pines" a capella at the school talent show, was descended from an English settler who died of a spider bite.

Japanese farmers brought strawberries to the Santa Maria Valley.

By the eve of the Second World War, Japanese farmers had become the primary strawberry-growers in the United States.

White farmers envied this success.

In 1942, President Franklin Roosevelt issued Executive Order 9066, forcing people of Japanese heritage to leave their homes, caging them in internment camps.

While the US waged war against Japan, white farmers usurped evacuated farms.

Due to Executive Order 9066, white farmers are now the primary growers of American strawberries.

According to the United Farm Workers, the piece-rate earning for strawberry harvesters is $2.50 per box.

According to the Santa Barbara County Agricultural Commissioner's Office, strawberry sales generated $775 million last year.

That's more than enough to buy everyone who harvests this fruit a house on a hill surrounded by beguiling oaks and sleepy bees.

A HUMAN BEEHIVE:
ZEKE BLATCHFORD OF YUCAIPE HAS A LIVELY EXPERIENCE

Los Angeles Herald, Sunday, May 21, 1893

Zeke Blatchford of Yucaipe...became a walking beehive last week. Having taken his noon lunch in the shade of a large boulder, he concluded to give a little time to a forty-wink nap. Sitting on a small stone, with his head resting comfortably against a soft spot on a big one, he dozed off, and when he awoke was considerably alarmed at finding a beehive started under his blouse near the small of his back....

TO BE

When I told Dad about the hive, he slid the phone book off its shelf and flipped to the yellow pages, skimming for beekeepers. I listened as he called one and scheduled an appointment for the honey expert to come and assess the situation on the hill.

The beekeeper huffed and puffed as he climbed our steep driveway.

"Hello!" he hollered "Hello!"

My brother and I sprinted toward him.

I slowed down when I realized he was old. Really old.

For some reason I thought he'd be young and dewy.

Instead, he looked like a pink mummy in denim overalls. He wore a pith hat with white netting.

At least he dressed the part.

He shook Dad's hand and in an ancient voice, asked, "Where's the bees?"

I volunteered, "I'll show you."

"No," said Dad. "I'll show him."

We watched our father escort the beekeeper onto the hill. They took careful steps, avoiding the drip irrigation's tubing and various saplings we'd planted. Dad pointed to the coyote brush. More insects had joined the community. They swarmed the shrub. Their humming was audible from yards away.

"Please stand back, sir," the beekeeper said to Dad.

Dad backed away.

The beekeeper carried a steel smoker that reminded me of the Tin Man. He aimed its spout at the insects and pumped the bellows. Thin wisps of smoke reached for the bees and the wisps grew, fattening into clouds that swirled around the hive. The scent seemed to calm the bees; it sang an olfactory lullaby. The beekeeper removed a canvas sack that was clipped to his belt. He opened it and, with his leathery hands, he loosened the hive and let it slide into the maw. After twisting the fabric shut, he walked the bees downhill, to the street. Standing at the rear of his truck, he released the tail gate, scooching a white box closer to himself. He transferred the disoriented contents of the canvas sack into the box, secured its lid, pushed it back into place, and then shut the gate.

"Is that it?" I asked.

The beekeeper laughed.

"That's it. You can go back to playing kickball now."

My brother went running to the garage to get a soccer ball.

I looked at the hill.

A straggler or two remained. Hmmmm...

I was curious about our bees.

Where had they gone?

When seemingly new bees appeared on the hill, shoving their faces into dandelions and roses, I'd ask, "Have we met before?"

Our native plants drew pollinators to the hill.

Western tiger swallowtails.

Yellowjackets.

Sweat bees.

Mexican free-tailed bats.

Anna's hummingbirds.

Sphinx moths.

Teddy-bear carpenter bees.

Most of California's native bees reject hive life. They're introverts. Rebels. Romantic hermits. Unlike European bees, they don't mind silence. Infinite lulls in the conversation.

Native bees can be found nesting in the ground or in tunnels burrowed by other insects.

Some native bees nap in flowers.

Female bees have abilities that male bees don't.

Stinging is one of these.

When European honeybees sting in self-defense, the act is suicidal.

The trauma may kill them.

When California native bees sting in self-defense, they live to tell the story but tell it to no one.

I was stung by a bee at a park.

I didn't see her there when I sat down.

She freaked out and attacked.

I cried when I felt her stinger go in because
    a) it hurt
    b) she died
    c) her death was my fault.

A month or two after our hive was removed, we went grocery shopping at Food 4 Less.

When we returned home, we pulled up the driveway and parked.

Dad bristled. "What the hell is that?" he muttered.

A glare. Sunlight reflected by glass.

I opened the van door and rushed to our porch.

Mason jars filled with amber.

A note attached.

From your bees...

LETTERS TO THE EDITOR: HALLOWEEN— TRICK OR TREAT FOR YOUNGSTERS?

Santa Maria Times, Monday, October 28, 1991

To the Editor:

Halloween is quickly approaching, and many are excitedly picking out costumes, planning parties, carving pumpkins and buying all kinds of treats for the kids.

As a born-again Christian of over thirty years, a true soldier in God's army and an adversary of the devil, my heart becomes very burdened every year as Halloween approaches!

While many are celebrating blindly this Satanic holiday, I become very aware of the sequence of events that are about to happen! I can no longer sit back while the world covers up these horrendous crimes with masks and candy!

THE HILL MONSTER

Once puberty changed my body, boys did things to me without my permission.

    Adults knew.

    They pretended not to.

Once puberty changed my body, men did things to me without my permission.

    Other adults knew.

    They pretended not to.

A trash bag.

A pillow.

A pillowcase.

A shotgun.

A handgun.

A knife.

A belt.

A shoe.

A book.

Silence.

Gossip.
Disbelief.

These are some of the weapons that boys and men have used to intimidate or hurt me.

The marijuana prince is all of these boys and all of these men past, present, and future.

The things that boys and men started doing to me when I turned twelve turned me into bitter fruit. This bitterness disrupted my relationship with the hill. My love for plants cooled. I was in pain and wanted it to stop. The pain distracted from everything. The pain colonized my attention. I became pain. Touching dirt no longer felt healing. The things that boys and men did to me made me feel a new type of dirty. I wanted for this type of dirty to be over.

I craved the right kind of dirty.
The right kind of dirty smells like fresh rain hitting playground earth.

Death represented my return to clean soil.

I committed myself to the aesthetics of lifelessness.

My wardrobe turned subterranean colors.

I decorated my bedroom with dry and decaying flowers.

Thistles.

The plants we'd planted remained outside my bedroom window, watching.

They knew what was happening.

They pressed leaves together, praying for me.

I unwittingly drew strength from their petitions.

Bats, bees, and beetles prayed for me too.

The hill monster drew strength from these same sources.

I was at home the afternoon that this creature emerged during daylight.

Step into my room...

I'm lying in my bed with Bram Stoker's *Dracula*.

Shrieking interrupts my reading pleasure.

I look up from the page.

I hear more shrieking.

It's my sister. It's definitely coming from my sister.

I see color.

Red.

A mirror reflects my face. I don't recognize it.

All I see is fury, fury in a long black dress, fury wearing black gloves, fury with black fingernail polish, fury in black boots.

I slide a bookmark into place and run to the front door.

After sprinting across the lawn, I stand at its edge, looking down across the hill.

I see my sister. A white boy holds her arms behind her back.

Two cowards stand off to the side, watching. Laughing.

A white boy is using my brother as his punching bag.

The hill monster awakens.

She levitates...

...speaks in long dormant tongues...

...soars as she wails...

...threatens the cruel boy with death.

The fool releases his victim.

The fool is trembling.

He shakes.

He begins to cry.

He's never seen a monster in real life.

Now, he's a believer.

The hill monster grabs the boy's neck.

She spins him in circles.

She strangles him.

Once Death caresses her victim's cheek, the monster loosens her grip.

She releases him.

She watches him run home.

Tired, she returns to the hill.

UNTITLED

Santa Maria Times, Saturday, July 22, 1893

Mrs. Blochman met with quite a serious accident last week by being thrown from a horse while botanizing in the Cuyama Mountains. No bones were broken, and she was able to ride home the next day.

EROSION

Last night, when I got back from watering the sequoias with my tears, I called my parents and asked if I could come see them.

They said, "Of course."

I figured they would.

I've missed them. I could hear in their voices that they've missed me too.

It's a beautiful day to go home. I haven't seen my parents in years and the weather is perfect for a three-hour drive.

That's how long it should take to get from my Bearbnb to the hill.

The sights along this long stretch of road remind me of a painting I saw in my high-school history textbook's chapter on the Great Depression. To illustrate the section on climate catastrophe, the editors chose *Drouth Stricken Area*, a painting by psychorealist Alexandre Hogue. It's part of his *Erosion* series.

"I was there," Hogue once explained to a curator, "not only while the Dust Bowl stage was being set but also when the curtain rose revealing its fury. I painted what I saw and experienced.... I did the Dust Bowl paintings because I was there before, during, and after the holocaust and could see the awesome, terrifying beauty of it with my own dust-filled eyes."

A dilapidated windmill teeters in the foreground of *Drouth Stricken Area*. A skeletal cow despairs. A vulture bides her time. Parched earth stretches to the horizon where beige blends with baby blue, a dreary Rothko. From behind a dirt dune peeks a farmhouse.

Dorothy Gale is trapped inside.

Will more bad weather be the spice of her life?

When I turned eighteen, I left home.

I thought that something was wrong with our valley.

In our valley, I kept getting hurt by boys and men.

Departure seemed a simple solution.

In my self-imposed exile, I ventured north.

For years, I lived in the city where Ida Mae Blochman gathered her final flowers. For years, I lived in the city where Lazar Blochman attempted to conjure the spirit of his pistol-packing ghost wife. A restless man, he bounced from residence to residence, arriving at 2239 Howe Street in 1938. That September, a reporter working for *The Oakland Post Enquirer* interviewed the former Santa Marian about his hobby, meteorology. Lazar explained that his interest in the weather could be traced to 1876, a year that San Francisco was very, very dry. When asked what to expect for the next few months, Lazar answered, "Rain—and plenty of it!" The reporter called the former Santa Marian "Berkeley's most famed weather prophet" and praised Lazar for being right about seventy-five percent of the time.

Lazar majored in geography and meteorology at the University of California at Berkeley. At age sixty-three, he earned his high school teacher's certificate.

What an overachiever.

Technically, I went to Berkeley to study.

Mostly, I wandered.

I wandered neighborhoods, past shingled houses haunted by Ida, Lazar, and ghost larkspur.

I haunted the campus at night.

Strawberry Creek drew me to its banks. The name attracted me. It reminded me of home.

At night, I tiptoed to the water. Once I was confident that I was alone, I sat beneath the stars. Bay laurels, sycamores, and oaks had lined Strawberry Creek before the university encroached. So had wild strawberries. Transplanted redwoods from Mendocino County replaced this native vegetation. The redwoods do okay at the creek. They would do better in a fog forest. Fog is their ice water. A necessary refreshment.

I sat at the foot of a redwood tree, doing my homework.
My English professor had assigned Salman Rushdie's monograph on *The Wizard of Oz*. I hadn't thought of Rushdie since fantasizing about exchanging his head for an infusion of cash into a college fund. As I read his essay about the film, I felt kind of bad about the homicidal thoughts I'd had as a child. At least I'd planned on spreading on the wealth.

Rushdie's essay taught me the phrase "authorless text." When I first read the phrase, I thought, "Yes, of course! That's what The Bible is!"
Rushdie's essay also taught me that when Dorothy says that there's no place like home, she's not talking about Kansas. She's talking about Oz.

I'm driving in the opposite direction from Kansas.

The landscape is softening.

Greening.

I'm going to Santa Maria, where the sun ripens like a strawberry and sinks gently into the sea.

SO WE'RE TOLD

The Berkeley Gazette, Monday, May 19, 1952

...we stopped at a luxurious motel in Santa Maria built far back enough from the highway so there was no truck and train obbligato. It is operated by a young Mormon couple from Utah. The husband explained that his wife's parents had just opened the place when both were killed in an auto accident.

They were greatly interested in what Hal told them about their own community—how the late L.E. Blochman, for many years a resident of Berkeley and the first long distance weather forecaster in the country, happened to leave Santa Maria. He was teaching school there and had a beautiful garden.

One morning he discovered his flowers ruined by seepage from the ground. It was oil...

SAMBUCUS MEXICANA

Mourning doves wake me.
  We're in Santa Maria.

At the kitchen table, we eat papaya, beans, and tortillas for breakfast. My mother, father, and I sip black coffee. I tell them about my day trip to Sequoia, that I journeyed there to see if the trees remembered me.
  "Did they remember that you stole something?" Dad asks.
  Mom laughs.
  "Yes. And I stole something new. A little gift for the hill monster."
  My father says, "After I finish using the toilet, I'll go with you to give it to him."

I have approximately fifteen minutes to kill.

Dad and I leave the house and walk across the lawn, to the entrance of a small dirt path that cuts through the grass, creating a trail. Lining it is a dense thicket of fried egg flowers, Matilija poppies, that sway. We take the trail. I ask, "When did the oaks get...so big?"
  These aren't the scrawny *Quercus agrifolia* of my childhood.

They're the oaks of my wet dreams. Robust. Gnarled. Burly. Rough. Twisted. Haggard.

A kinky grove.

"I don't know. Years ago. You know, it's a myth that it takes oaks forever to grow. Some oaks do. Not these though."

We inhaled the gift that the oaks exhaled. Oxygen.

We felt at home.

We let our legs rest.

Dad pointed at a plant I hadn't seen on the hill before.

"Do you recognize that?"

"Elderberry?"

"Yes."

"Do you know how it got here?"

"Did we plant it?"

"No..." Dad quieted.

"How did it get here?"

Dad seemed to glow as he explained the tree's arrival. He reminded me that we'd tried to plant elderberries but that they never survived. They got sad and died. Watching so many elderberries give up on life made Dad give up on planting them. Then, one day when he was out cutting oak branches, he noticed that a seedling had sprouted. It was the elderberry. Dad looked at the sky and said, "I think my father sent it. He asked a bird to drop seeds here. He loved elderberry wine."

I smiled at the elderberry. Then, I slid the pebble I'd stolen from Sequoia and placed it at her feet.

"That's your gift for the hill monster?"

"Yeah."

We walked the entire loop as Dad talked more about the cheerful grapevines and agaves.

Oaks and Catalina ironwoods towered. They listened.

Before I leave, I stand alone in the oak grove that we created, the same oak grove that recreates me.

OUR WILDFLOWERS:
A DESCRIPTION OF OUR OAKS AND
THEIR ORNAMENTAL MOSS

Santa Maria Times, Saturday, December 17, 1892

So far as I know there are only two kinds of oak trees in this vicinity. By far the more common one is our so-called "Live Oak," the Quercus agrifolia *of botanists. It grows everywhere in our canyons and on our hillsides and its short trunk and wide stretched branches are too familiar to need description. It has a most unfortunate habit of leaning inland which might lead those unacquainted with our climate to suppose we have "exceptional" days...*

VITAL GARNISH

The drive to my apartment was citrus-scented. A few years ago, Dad planted a lemon tree for mom, and her branches were heavy with fruit. Half of her lemons rode home with me. They jostled in paper grocery bags in the back seat, inspiring fantasies of lemon meringue, lemon curd, and lemonade.

Lemons can also be used in banishment rituals.

I can't share every step that a witch takes with fruit to get rid of someone, but I will share five.

1) Using a No. 2 pencil, write the name of the person to be exiled on a strip of brown paper.

2) Roll the paper tightly, creating a slender mummy.

3) Use the pencil to create a tunnel from the lemon's rind to her center.

4) Insert the paper into the lemon.

5) Squeeze.

It doesn't get much worse than a lemon juice bath.

When I got home, I lugged my lemons upstairs, opened my front door, and elbowed my way inside, making my way through bushy corn that was now a foot taller than me. I set the lemons down in my kitchen and then walked from room to room, inspecting. Happy plants greeted me in the bathroom. Happy plants greeted me in my bedroom. Happy plants greeted me in my dining room.

Hungry, I decided to eat.

I plucked an ear of corn in my living room and shucked it over the sink. On the windowsill, my poppy bloomed, exposing her globular ovary. Her petals are epic. The color of radioactive nacho cheese.

"I see you," I said.

She bloomed even harder, quivering.

I roasted my elote on the comal. listening to her sizzle and pop. She had a lot to say. Corn mostly speaks in *s* sounds when she's being cooked.

Sssss, pop.

Sssss.

Once her kernels had crisped, I plated her. I cut one of Mom's lemons in half and squirted juice on the cob, drenching her. Then, I slathered some butter and chile across her too. My mouth watered.

My corn was missing a vital garnish.

With scissors, I clipped the poppy. I carried her to the dining room table, where my elote waited between calendula and sunflowers. I sat down, said a prayer, and plucked her petals, letting them fall on the kernels. Their hue darkened, becoming a richer carotene.

Bite by bite, I ate my corn.

Bite by bite, I ate my poppy.

Bite by bite, I ate my lemon.

Bite by bite, I ate my butter.

Bite by bite, I ate my chile.

Bite by bite, I became myself again.

A poppy.

Corn.

Author's Note

POPPY STATE is a metaphorical habitat. It uses the structure of a labyrinthine secret garden, ushering the reader through a compendium of anecdotes, reminiscences, utterances, lists, incantations, newspaper articles, and other ephemera, ultimately shaping a maze through accretion, repetition, and occasional surprise.

POPPY STATE invites readers to meditate on the following questions.

How does one ethically inhabit land?

How does one ethically inhabit one's own body?

How do we ethically inhabit this planet together?

The last question is for all species.

POPPY STATE is a book-length condemnation of settler-colonialism. My family members, both native and non-native, are the actors animating my analyses. They are the figures through which I connect to the soil and, thusly, to plants.

POPPY STATE is about soul loss. Absence is its foundation. After surviving sublethal misogynist violence on several occasions, my terrified soul left my body. This condition is called susto, and to retrieve my soul I had to right my relationship with myself. That required me to mend my relationship with soil and plants. By caring for plants, I began a process of restoration. Plants mentored me in reciprocity, reminding me that if we do for them, they will do for us. If I do for my body, as if she, too, is the earth, my soul may thrive in the home that I make for her, just as a plant would.

POPPY STATE is a multicursal puzzle punctuated by "dead ends." Time functions differently when one is lost, and when readers find themselves in these dead ends, they are urged to stop, rest, and wonder.

POPPY STATE is influenced by Jorge Luis Borges's *Labyrinths: Selected Stories and Other Writings*. "The Garden of Forking Paths" prompted me to spin my own web: "I thought of a labyrinth of labyrinths, of one sinuous spreading labyrinth that would encompass the past and future and in some way involve the stars. Absorbed in these illusory images, I forgot my destiny of one pursued. I felt myself to be, for an unknown period of time, an abstract perceiver of the world." While the structure of the book is Borgean, POPPY STATE stylistically borrows from *Wisconsin Death Trip*, a 1999 docudrama about the horror of Midwestern life.

POPPY STATE was written communally. I composed it with my ancestors, to and with whom I regularly prayed at my home altars. I also spoke with my father as I was writing it. He and I reminisced about our days gardening together. Plants, animals, and rocks also worked with me. On days that I wrote, I would go for walks in the Angeles National Forest, where I would visit the beings that I was writing about—oaks, crows, elderberries, sycamores. I harvested acorns, flowers, berries, and twigs, and brought them home. I offered these friends gifts and invited them to tell stories. They did.

Table Of Contents

Because a table of contents cannot be created for a maze, I offer maize in its place.

Acknowledgments

POPPY STATE was shaped, crafted, and written by so many. I'm grateful to Makenna Goodman for championing this project and guiding me through the editorial process. Mina Hamedi, you're amazing. I'm profoundly appreciative of historian Rocio Moreno, comunera del Pueblo Coca de Mezcala, for the work she has done on behalf of indigenous communities living in southern Jalisco. Blessings upon my madrina and ilé. Flowers for those who took the time to explore with me the ideas that came to form this labyrinth: Loma, Griz, Diana, Alán, Amrah, Henry, Desi, Allison, Tiombe, Wendy, and Karla. Most importantly, gracias a la Tierra.